LLŶN HILLS

Carreg C

WAI̧ ̧E
LLŶN HILLS

Des Marshall

Mynydd Enlli

NV VISAFSLAG URK

Snowdon from Gyrn Ddu with Gyrn Goch on the left

First published in 2017

ISBN: 978-1-84524-266-4

Cover design: Carreg Gwalch
Cover image: Llŷn from Mynydd Enlli

Published by Gwasg Carreg Gwalch,
12 Iard yr Orsaf, Llanrwst, Wales LL26 0EH
tel: 01492 642031
fax: 01492 641502
email: books@carreg-gwalch.com
website: www.carreg-gwalch.com

Yr Eifl (Garn Ganol)

Garn Fadryn from Garn Bach

3

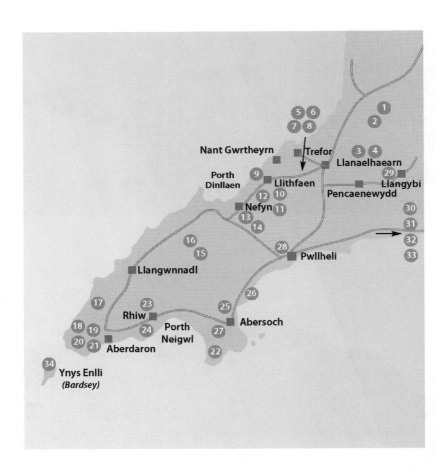

Contents

Tre'r Ceiri – a Celtic hillfort

Introduction

Although not as high as the mountains of Snowdonia these hills have the feel of being just as high. Many ascents are long and steep. However, the rewards for persevering are magnificent views from just about every summit, especially those from Yr Eifl (mistranslated as 'the rivals' in earlier days) and Bwlch Mawr. It is a wonderful area being designated an Area of Outstanding Natural Beauty. The weather is often much better than Snowdonia with the hills being basked in sunshine when Snowdonia is experiencing monsoon conditions. In winter snow and frost are the exception although snow does fall in some winters. However, snow on the hills on the summits in Snowdonia makes for breath-taking viewing. Because of the proximity of the coast the hills seem much higher. There are areas that are remote and it is easy to find solitude in these hills.

The guide is intended to catalogue all the hills on the peninsula. I have used the A487 as the eastern boundary and Caernarfon as the northern. A list of hills has been included and indicates which hills can be climbed. A few walks are very short indeed being less than a mile. Some hills have no access even those supposedly lying on access land as there seems to be no way to reach it. In all there are 34 walks for the 40 accessible summits. Because the area is not as frequently walked as the mountains in Snowdonia paths are often faint or non-existing. It is therefore necessary to be able to map read and use a compass. However, GPS devices are now gaining in popularity but they are only as good as their batteries!

There are two maps that cover the area and these

are the Ordnance Survey the 1:25,000 Explorer series number 254 Llŷn Peninsula East/Pen Llŷn Ardal Ddwyreiniol and 253 Llŷn Peninsula West/Pen Llŷn Ardal Orllewinol. These maps have much greater detail than the Ordnance Survey Landranger 1:50,000 series although this does give an overall picture of the peninsula. The one covering the area is number 123 Llŷn Peninsula/Pen Llŷn.

The Llŷn peninsula, a long finger of land stretching some 30 miles out into the Irish Sea, is the northern boundary of Cardigan Bay and divides it from Caernarfon Bay. For much of its length the width is only 8 miles. It has sea on three sides and there are views to it from all the summits, although for a few it is somewhat distant. The peninsula can be taken as a line drawn from Caernarfon to Porthmadog although many say that the true peninsula is a line drawn from Clynnog Fawr to Cricieth (the correct Welsh spelling). The coastline of the peninsula is almost 100 miles and the Coastal Path is a superb walk. There are many secret coves and dramatic headlands especially at Cilan Head which lends itself to some very adventurous rock climbing.

Ynys Enlli (*Bardsey*) is almost 2 miles offshore from Mynydd Mawr and I have regarded this as part of the peninsula. As such Mynydd Enlli is included in the walks. People have lived on the island since Neolithic times. During the 5th century it was a sanctuary for persecuted Christians. St Cadfan (who founded the church in Tywyn) came to the island in 516 and under his guidance St Mary's Abbey was built. He was the first abbot on the island from 516 to 542. King Arthur reigned during this period. He had a sister called Gwenonwy whose name was given to Maen

Gwenonwy, a rocky island at Porth Cadlan. She married Gwyndaf Hen (he is buried on Ynys Enlli) and they had a son called Hywyn who became the patron saint of the church at Aberdaron. For many centuries Ynys Enlli was regarded as a land of indulgencies, absolution and pardon on the way to Heaven and the gateway to Paradise. It is rumoured that 20,000 Saints are buried on the island, however this can, possibly, be attributed to the fact that elderly monks retreated here near the end of their lives and possibly could be classed as such. Three pilgrimages to Ynys Enlli were the equivalent of one to Rome!

The history of the Llŷn peninsula is indeed a long one. There are numerous wells dotted around the peninsula with many dating back to the pre-Christian era. Many have holy connotations and they were important stops for pilgrims heading to Ynys Enlli. One such well on the tip of the peninsula is called St Mary's and can be reached by a scramble for the confident. Maen Melyn, a prehistoric monolite on the cliff top, was named after its 'yellow' colour, is mentioned in Welsh medieval poetry and was used as a crossing marker by pilgrims to and from Enlli. Another well at Clynnog Fawr can be seen without walking and is called St Beuno's. Another, needing an easy short walk to it, is St Cybi's. This is in a good state of preservation. Notes about these are indicated in the text along with many other interesting facts pertaining to each particular walk.

Llŷn is basically a rural area and is characterised by small houses, cottages and small farms. The villages tend to be compact and built from the local stone as seen by the many stone quarries. The only larger scale industry were quarrying and mining. Manganese was mined close to Porth Ysgo and at Rhiw between 1894 and 1945. Stone from the Garn Fôr quarry was used to make the curling stones for the 2006 Turin Winter Olympics. Other minerals were also mined such as lead, copper and zinc. Shipbuilding was also an important industry notably at Nefyn, Aberdaron and Abersoch. In the 18th and 19th centuries over 400 ships were built in Pwllheli. Sadly the industry collapsed after the introduction of steel ships in 1880. Nefyn was an important herring fishing port whilst other coastal communities fished for crab and lobster.

Originally farming was very simple and wholly organic. Unfortunately major changes were introduced after the Second World War. Machines came into use, land was drained and fields seeded. Artificial fertilisers, herbicides and pesticides were introduced after 1950 leading to some quite stark changes in the appearance to the countryside.

Perhaps the main industry today is tourism. The railway arrived in Pwllheli in 1867 and the town expanded rapidly. A tramway was built linking the town to Llanbedrog. After World War II, Billy Butlin established a holiday camp at Penychain. Called Butlins it is now known as Hafan y Môr. He established his first camp in Skegness in 1936.

The geology of Llŷn is complex. The majority of the rock on the peninsula is volcanic from the Ordovician period whilst rock of Cambrian origin occurs south of Abersoch. Many granite intrusions and outcrops form the prominent hills such as Yr Eifl. Gabbro can be found at the west end of Porth Neigwl. The western part of the peninsula (north-west of a line drawn from Nefyn to Aberdaron) is formed from Pre-Cambrian rocks. The majority of these are thought to form a part of the Monian Complex making them closely related to rock found on Anglesey. There are many faults in the area and a major shear zone. This is known as the Llŷn Shear Zone and runs northeast to southwest through the Monian rocks. In 1984 there was an earthquake beneath the peninsula measuring 5.4 on the Richter Scale. It was felt as far away as Ireland.

There is much to interest the bird watcher and botanists. The headlands are home to the chough one of Britain's rarest birds although very often seen. The chough is regarded as Llŷn's bird and a few circular symbols can still be seen in several places. Choughs have distinctive red legs and a red bill as well as being very black and glossy. A member of the crow family it is an acrobatic bird with a mewing cry confirming its identity. There are around 100 nesting pairs on the Llŷn due to the ideal breeding conditions, short grass, a rocky coastline, caves and a temperate climate. In Cornish legend King Arthur did not die at Camlan, his last battle. His soul migrated into the body of a chough with the red bill and legs supposedly derived from the blood of that battle. It is said that it is unlucky to kill this bird.

There are many other birds such as buzzards, peregrines, ravens, guillemots and fulmars. Other birds frequently seen are stonechats, linnets, whitethroats and willow warblers. Puffins are known to nest and an exotic visitor, the hoopoe is occasionally seen. There is a seabird sanctuary on Ynys Enlli. It shelters the Manx shearwaters and puffins.

The common mammals seen here include badgers and foxes with a healthy population of brown hares. Occasionally polecats can be seen as well as weasels and stoats. Grey seals, harbour porpoises with both bottle-nosed and Risso's dolphins frequently seen.

Many wild flowers adorn the landscape throughout the year due to the mild climate. The headlands are home to beautiful gorse and heather. Where flowering together it is a most wonderful sight, an absolute riot of purple and gold. The very rare spotted rock rose can only be found in one localised area. It flowers only for a few hours before the petals drop off. Spring squill, green-winged orchid and the rare prostrate broom are also found on the peninsula.

Because of the abundance of flowers there is also an interesting array of insects. These include the glow-worm, green tiger beetle and the minotaur beetle. This has large horns resembling a miniature triceratops. Butterfly species include the dark-green fritillary and the rare marsh fritillary. There are also day time flying moths such as the emperor and the amazing scarlet tiger.

Llŷn is a very welcoming and special place. As such I would recommend a visit for any walker especially if wanting to avoid the hordes in Snowdonia, not to mention the frequent bad weather those mountains attract.

Llŷn Peninsula List of Hills

HILL	HEIGHT IN METRES	MAP REFERENCE	DATE ASCENDED
GARN GANOL (YR EIFL)	564	SH 3650 4474	
GYRN DDU	522	SH 4015 4675	
BWLCH MAWR	509	SH 4266 4785	
GYRN GOCH	492	SH 4073 4751	
TRE'R CEIRI	485	SH 3743 4470	
GARN FÔR	444	SH 3610 4572	
MOEL BRONMIOD	416	SH 4121 4554	
PEN Y GAER	389	SH 4289 4552	

Summit is on access land but there is no public footpath to it

HILL	HEIGHT IN METRES	MAP REFERENCE	DATE ASCENDED
GARN FADRYN	371	SH 2785 3517	
MYNYDD CARNGUWCH	359	SH 3745 4290	
MOEL PEN-LLECHOG	316	SH 3891 4601	

*Summit is on access land but there is no public footpath to it
and only accessible by climbing loose high walls*

HILL	HEIGHT IN METRES	MAP REFERENCE	DATE ASCENDED
MYNYDD RHIW	304	SH 2285 2937	
GARN BACH	281	SH 2855 3460	
GARN BODUAN	279	SH 3113 3936	
CLIP Y GYLFINIR	270	SH 2239 2848	
MYNYDD CENNIN	262	SH 4583 4496	

Summit is on access land but there is no public footpath to it

HILL	HEIGHT IN METRES	MAP REFERENCE	DATE ASCENDED
MOEL Y GEST	262	SH 5495 3894	
CARREGLEFAIN	261	SH 3242 4109	
MYNYDD NEFYN	256	SH 3249 4065	
MYNYDD Y GRAIG	242	SH 2281 2744	
MOELFRE	240	SH 3939 4466	

No public path or access

HILL	HEIGHT IN METRES	MAP REFERENCE	DATE ASCENDED
GWYLWYR	237	SH 3205 4125	
MOEL GWYNUS	236	SH 3407 4229	

*Summit on private land. Reachable high point is only a foot or
so lower a few feet away and has the same views*

CARNEDDOL	235	SH 3014 3310

No public path or access

CARN SAETHON	230	SH 2982 3370

Summit is on access land but there is no public path to it

GARN BENTYRCH	228	SH 4223 4189

*Summit is on private land but lower one of 222m with trig point
can be reached by public path. A wonderful view*

FOEL	221	SH 4500 5067

No public path or access

Y FOEL	218	SH 4647 4665

Summit on private land and not on a public footpath

MOEL TÎ-GWYN	217	SH 3320 4166
MOEL CAERAU	207	SH 2923 3548
MYNYTHO COMIN	194	SH 2986 3189
MYNYDD ANELOG	192	SH 1519 2721
FOEL FAWR	c190	SH 3055 3218
MYNYDD CEFNAMWLCH		
WEST PEAK	182	SH 2266 3389

It is not possible to reach the summit due to impenetrable undergrowth

BRYNIAU YSTUMCEGID	179	SH 5036 4193

No public access

MYNYDD PENARFYNYDD	177	SH 2203 2659
BRYN BRAICH-Y-SAINT	176	SH 5143 4052
MYNYDD CEFNAMWLCH		
EAST PEAK	175	SH 2297 3390
FOEL GRON	c175	SH 3014 3108
MYNYDD ENLLI	167	SH 1228 2193
BRYN HYWEL	159	SH 5151 4177
MOELYPENMAEN	153	SH 3381 3868

On access land but no public path or access to it

MYNYDD MAWR	151	SH 1403 2592
RHOS-DU	150	SH 2556 3479

No public path or access

MYNYDD YSTUM	146	SH 1871 2848

MOEL EDNYFED	136	SH 5023 3938

Access is via golf club road from Cricieth,
NOT as marked on map up Nant y Wyddan

MYNYDD TIRYCWMWD	133	SH 3290 3091
MYNYDD CILAN	117	SH 2886 2421
MYNYDD BYCHESTYN		
(PEN Y CIL)	107	SH 1561 2430
CLOGWYN BACH	103	SH 3858 3711
MYNYDD GWYDDEL	99	SH 1420 2519
MYNYDD CARREG	92	SH 1637 2916
COED MYNYDD-MEILIAN	90	SH 2953 3713

No public path or access and densely forested

PEN Y GAER	80	SH 2986 2823

Not on a public footpath but there appears to be no access problems

PEN Y GARN	71	SH 3705 3535
MOEL Y GADAIR	67	SH 5220 3914

No public path or access

Garn Boduan

*Snowdon from
the summit of
Bwlch Mawr*

Bwlch Mawr

Walk details

Height:	*509 metres, Grid Ref. SH 4266 4785*
Distance:	*5 miles*
Time:	*3½ hours*
O.S. Maps:	*1:25,000 Explorer Sheet 254 or 1:50,000 Landranger Sheet 123*
Start:	*Car park in the centre of Clynnog Fawr opposite the large white building, that was once the Coach Inn Grid Ref. SH 4151 497*
Access:	*Follow the A499 to Clynnog Fawr and turn into the village*
Parking:	*Free car park in the centre*
Notes:	*Superb views. This is a strenuous high mountain walk. Care is needed on the vegetated descent through the wood*
Going:	*Road and track at the start then paths to reach the open hillside. The walk is then virtually pathless until entering the wood during the descent. This is vegetated and quite slippery in wet weather across a steep hillside to reach easier going through a wood on a track. This is followed to the road leading back to the start*

This is a wonderful, not to be missed, 5 miles walk. It feels big and compares very favourably with many

Penygroes and Talysarn from Bwlch Mawr

walks in the high mountains of Snowdonia. It is also quite strenuous. However, the views from the summit are some of the best around being eclipsed only by those from Yr Eifl. Once the wall close to the summit is left behind paths are non-existent until, thankfully, one is descended through the wood to reach the A499. NOTE that care is needed on the initial descent through the wood, especially in wet weather when the going becomes somewhat treacherous.

The dominant feature of Clynnog Fawr is the huge church, dedicated to St Beuno and is much bigger than one would expect in a village of this size. The church dates mostly from the 15th and 16th centuries and is reputedly situated on the site of a Celtic Monastery founded by Saint Beuno in the early 7th century. Clynnog means 'the place of holly trees'. The original church was burnt down twice, firstly by the Vikings in 978 and secondly by the Normans. In the 15th century it became a collegiate church, one of only six in Wales. Clynnog is on the Taith Pererin or

Pilgrim's Way from Saint Winefride's Well at Basingwerk Abbey, Holywell to Aberdaron from where the pilgrims sailed to Ynys Enlli (Bardsey). Because of this it was an important stopping off place. The upright sundial in the churchyard is dated between the 10th and 12th centuries. It is an Anglo-Saxon type with its purpose to mark the time of the canonical hours. A wooden chest, Cyff Beuno, seen in the church was used to keep alms donated by the pilgrims as well as from the sale of lambs and calves that were sold by the churchwardens. The chest is believed to date from the middle ages and the padlocks date from around 1600. It has not always been peaceful hereabouts as a number of battles have been fought in the area. In 1075 the Battle of Bron yr Erw took place when Gruffudd ap Cynan made his first bid to become King of Gwynedd but was defeated by Trahaearn ap Caradog. The 1255 Battle of Bryn Derwin broke out when Llywelyn ap Gruffudd defeated his brothers Owain and Dafydd to become the sole ruler of Gwynedd.

To the right of the old Coach Inn, dated 1912, walk up the narrow lane on the immediate left of the old Post Office up to and over a cattle grid at a left hand hairpin bend. Turn right at the bridleway sign 30 metres further. Follow the steadily rising path and go through a gate. Go up the path with a stream on the right. The path itself becomes a stream in wet weather! Continue up to a marker post, still with the stream to the right. Cross a short but very boggy section and continue up and through the metal waymarked gate. The path becomes boggy again and continues to pass through another waymarked old metal gate. Keep following the path with the stream on the right. Pass through a gap in the wall and turn immediately to the right at the marker post. Continue up to go through another waymarked old metal gate. Keep following the path again with the stream on the right at first to another waymarked metal gate. Pass through to a cottage on the right. *Note the old waterwheel on the gable end.*

Continue up with the stream on the left to cross a boggy section just before reaching a gate. The path often doubles as a stream itself in wet weather! Go through the gate to the marker post. Bear left and up the left edge of the field still with the stream on the left. Pass through a waymarked gate on the left just before some sheep pens. Turn right and go up to a waymarked gate. Go through this into a field. Walk up this with a wall and fence to the right and a very low wall to left. There is a great view of Gyrn Goch 492 metres and behind over to Anglesey. Go through a gap in the low wall close to the top of the field and continue up to a kissing-gate and gate.

Pass through either. Bear up and slightly left towards the left hand rocky peak. Although it appears to be the summit it is not as this is beyond it. Pick the easiest line between the stunted gorse bushes. As the gorse is left behind the way is littered with small rocks but it is easy to find a way to weave between them. Once clear of these bear left across grass to a wall. Cross this carefully but quite easily some 20 metres before the wall going up the hill. Continue up on the obvious narrow, grassy path to the trig point and amazing views.

The main mountains seen are Snowdon 1,085 metres, Moel Hebog 782 metres, the Moelwynion and Aran mountains on the very far eastern skyline as well as the Rhinogydd and Cadair Idris 893 metres. Nearer are the Llŷn hills of Gyrn Goch 492 metres, Gyrn Ddu 522 metres with Garn Ganol 564 metres, beyond these.

Retrace steps to and over the wall. Bear due west over stony ground to where a wall bounding the forest below comes into view. Descend to the left hand corner of

Aberdesach from Bwlch Mawr

this at SH 4150 4778. Keeping the wall to the right descend to a marker post just before the tumbling Afon Hen. Pass through the kissing-gate on the right and descend to another marker post. Turn right as indicated and ascend slightly then along to the next marker post. Continue CAREFULLY across the steep vegetated slope gradually descending to the next marker post. From this an easier path descends to reach a track. Follow this down to another marker post and bear left through conifers and bearing right to go through a waymarked gate.

Follow the track down to the A499. Turn right along the cycle way/path to Clynnog Fawr. Just before entering the village is Ffynnon Beuno – St Beuno's well.

It was customary for the sick to bathe in the waters and then be carried to St Beuno's chapel to spend the night resting on top of Beuno's tomb hoping for a cure!

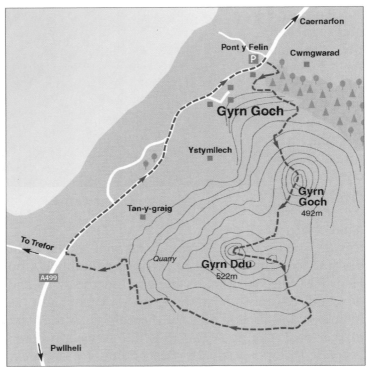

Trefor and pier from Gyrn Ddu

Walk 2
Gyrn Goch and Gyrn Ddu

Walk details

Height: *Gyrn Goch 492 metres, Grid Ref. SH 4073 4751*
           Gyrn Ddu 522 metres, Grid Ref. SH 4015 4675

Distance: *6½ miles*

Time: *4 hours*

O.S. Maps: *1:25,000 Explorer Sheet 254 or*
           1:50,000 Landranger Sheet 123

Start: *In the village of Gyrn Goch by the old bridge*
           Grid Ref. SH 4046 4867

Access: *Follow the A499 to Gyrn Goch and turn into the*
           loop of road by the bridge. Up the signed bridleway
           on left of Afon Hen

Parking: *Free car parking close to bridge*

Notes: *Superb views. This is a strenuous high mountain*
           walk needing care with some scrambling. It is
           largely guided by walls

Going: *There is a track and path at the start. The pathless*
           ascent of Gyrn Goch is on steep grass which ends at
           a short easy scramble to gain the summit. After a
           short wet section the final ascent of Gyrn Ddu is a
           scramble over boulders and an equally awkward
           boulder descent back down to grass. A grassy
           descent is then made alongside a wall to a track.
           This leads to a path which goes down to the road
           which is followed back to the start

This is another of those wonderful, not to be missed, walks. It feels big and compares very favourably with many walks in the high mountains of Snowdonia. It is also strenuous. However, the views from the summit are superb. Initially from the start the way is easy to follow along paths. However, having turned right from the gate close to the forest there are no more paths although the wall leads directly to the summit of Gyrn Goch. Vague paths are followed close to a wall to the rough scramble, where care is needed on the sometimes loose huge boulders, up to the summit of Gyrn Ddu. A path can be followed after the rocky descent from summit of Gyrn Ddu to the subsidiary summit. The descent alongside the wall from here leads to a sheep pen where a path can be followed back to the road at SN 3861 4676. The section from Gyrn Goch to Gyrn Ddu seems remote and isolated.

When travelling from Pwllheli and just before the speed de-restriction signs when leaving the tiny village of Gyrn Goch or just after them coming from the Caernarfon direction, there is a bridge over Afon Hen and bridleway sign.

Follow the path up with the track and Afon Hen to the right. Cross the track and continue up to and through a waymarked gate.

Looking back to Gyrn Goch from Gyrn Ddu

Continue to cross the waymarked footbridge over the stream. Follow the wide path to the right past a waymark and go up to the next marker post. Bear right to go over the fine waymarked stone step stile. Continue up to a gate and marker post (there is also a marker post for the Taith Pererin). DO NOT go through but go up to the left and follow the path slanting up and across the hillside to a wall. Follow the path up through a short walled section onto the open hillside. Continue up the path to a gate set in the wall.

DO NOT go through this gate. Turn right and follow the wall steeply up keeping it to the left to where it turns 90 degrees up to the left. Turn left with it and continue more steeply to a short steep scramble. Climb easily over the wall by a very convenient boulder to reach the summit and crowning cairn. There are superb views from here.

Views extend from Snowdon 1,085 metres, the Nantlle Ridge, Moel Hebog 782 metres, the Moelwynion, the Rhinogydd whilst further down is Cadair Idris 893 metres. Gyrn Ddu, 522 metres, is the next hill to be climbed and presents a fine pyramidal form. Yr Eifl (The Rivals), Tre'r Ceiri 485 metres, Garn Ganol 564 metres and Garn Fôr 444 metres are seen to the right, Trefor is the village and obvious pier below Garn Fôr.

Trefor owes its existence to the stone quarries on Yr Eifl, in particular on Garn Fôr, 444 metres, whilst the harbour was constructed for easy shipment. The granite like stone extracted from the huge quarry was used for kerb stones and 'setts' (small stone blocks or cobbles) in the cities of England and Wales. It is extremely hard wearing and is composed of porphyrite and quartz. Making 'setts' was a great skill that entailed a 3 years apprenticeship. Stone extracted from here was used to make the curling stones for the 2006 Winter Olympics in Turin. Wagons carried the stone down a cable controlled incline to the harbour. Samuel Holland started the quarry which prospered in the middle of the 19th century. At one time some 800 men worked in this quarry, the largest one of all in the area. Trefor was named after Trevor Jones, Holland's foreman.

From the summit follow the wall down keeping it to the right into the dip. Keep following the wall to the right to go through a gap in it just after it has turned leftwards. Continue towards the rocky summit of Gyrn Ddu and cross a short but boggy section to reach large boulders guarding the summit. The boulder scramble demands CARE as some of the boulders are loose. A large cairn adorns the summit rocks.

There is an 'unrivalled' view of Yr Eifl from here! Llanaelhaearn is the village seen below and left of Tre'r Ceiri.

Descend the boulders CAREFULLY heading eastwards to a grassy area where there is a path. Follow this past a shelter/ruin going along and up to spot height 491 metres. There is a giant cairn in front of the wall! Pass in front of the cairn and descend 25 metres to go through a gap in the wall, there are several so choose the easiest. Descend with the wall to the right to a sheepfold and ladder stile on the left of a gate. The ladder stile is in a state of disrepair so go through the gate.

Continue with the wall to the right and through a gateless gap (ruined stile on the left). Follow the wall, now to the left, to reach a ladder stile. This one is OK so climb over it. The path is now a grassy track and continues over another ladder stile immediately before a building over to the left. Pass through another gateless gap (with, strangely a ladder stile to the left).

Ascend slightly with the wall to the right and pass through a walled section to reach some sheepfolds with a marker post on the left. Continue now with a fence to the right to a

Looking towards Moel Bronmiod

kissing-gate. Pass through this and follow the path/track down past ruins for an old stone quarry. Zigzag down the track until 100 metres from a wall ahead and an obvious pointed rock.

The track bears right here. Continue straight ahead down the path past the pointed rock. Keep following the path down past a marker post and metal clad shed. Turn right through a kissing-gate 10 metres beyond the shed. Turn left and cross the field to a wall. Follow this to the left to go through a kissing-gate by a marker post to reach a track. Turn right down this to the A499. Turn right and follow the cycleway/path back into Gyrn Goch for 1¾ miles, or if the timing is right catch the bus. If two cars are available one can be left here on the old section of road being careful not to block the turning for Rock Cottage. There is bus stop with a timetable on the far side of the busy A499 almost opposite where the path joins the cycleway/path.

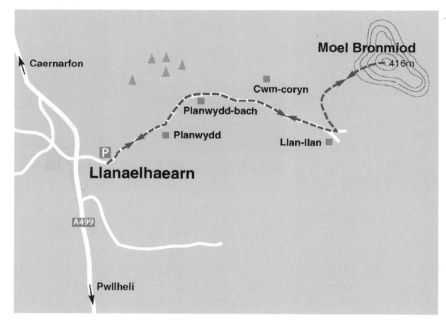

Summit of Moel Bronmiod

Moel Bronmiod

Walk details

Height:	*416 metres, Grid Ref. SH 4121 4554*
Distance:	*4¼ miles*
Time:	*2½ hours*
O.S. Maps:	*1:25,000 Explorer Sheet 254 or 1:50,000 Landranger Sheet 123*
Start:	*From the layby 250 metres up the dead-end minor road leaving Llanaelhaern Grid Ref. SH 3918 4475*
Access:	*Follow the A499 to Llanaelhaern and turn up the dead-end minor road*
Parking:	*Free car parking at the layby*
Notes:	*Great views*
Going:	*A gentle road walk leads to a rough track. This is followed to where a steep, grassy and pathless ascent leads to the summit*

This is a good linear walk to an outlying peak in the Gyrn Ddu range. Although not as high as others hereabouts, it is a very fine viewpoint. The narrow road at the start and finish only serves the farms along it. As such it is very quiet. Parking is possible in the village of Llanaelhaearn, but there is a large layby on the narrow road. It is found on the left 250 metres after leaving the village where it is possible to park 3 or 4 cars.

Walk up the road until just before the tarmac ends. Here a track branches off to the left. Follow this for 40 metres and go through the gate. There is a waymark on the gate post at the far side! Follow the track as it bends to the left and rises gently to pass through another gate. Turn right off the track 10 metres further on and go up keeping to the left of the sheep pens.

Once past these continue up keeping the wall to the right to where it turns 90 degrees to the right. Continue straight up bearing slightly left to reach a very broad, grassy ridge. Continue up this bearing right to the rocky summit. Just below this is a small stone shelter.

There is a very fine panoramic view from the summit. Moel Hebog 782 metres, the Moelwynion and Aran mountains, Rhinogydd, Cadair Idris 893 metres and the huge sweep of Cardigan Bay to the east and south. To the south west is mynydd Carnguwch. To the west are Yr Eifl (The Rivals) right to left these are Tre'r Ceiri 485 metres, Garn Ganol 564 metres and Garn Fôr 444 metres whilst northward are the more remote hills of Gyrn Ddu 522

metres and Gyrn Goch 492 metres with Bwlch Mawr 509 metres on the right of these. Snowdon, 1,085 metres is visible to the left of Moel Hebog.

Return to the layby by reversing the outward walk.

Pen y Gaer form Moel Bronmiod

Walk 4
Pen y Gaer (Moel Bronmiod)

Walk details

Height: 389 metres, Grid Ref. SH 4289 4552

Distance: 6¼ miles

Time: 4 hours

O.S. Maps: 1:25,000 Explorer Sheet 254 or
                     1:50,000 Landranger Sheet 123

Start: From the layby 250 metres up the dead-end minor
                     road leaving Llanaelhaern
                     Grid Ref. SH 3918 4475

Access: Follow the A499 to Llanaelhaern and turn up the
                     dead-end road

Parking: Free car parking at the layby

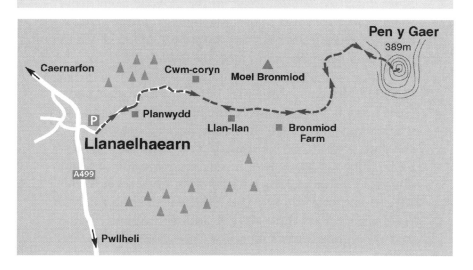

Notes: *Great views. Please keep to way described. There is much private land around here*

Going: *A gentle road walk leads to a rough track. This is followed to a steep and grassy pathless ascent to the fort on the summit*

This is a good linear walk to another outlying peak in the Gyrn Ddu range. Although not as high as others hereabouts, only reaching 385 metres, it is a very fine viewpoint with the remains of Iron Age hillfort close to the summit. There is an air of remoteness when the walk enters the basin below Gyrn Ddu 522 metres and on to the final uphill section to the wall of the fort and summit. The narrow road at the start and finish only serves the farms along it. As such it is very quiet. Parking is possible in the village of Llanaelhaearn, but there is a large layby on the narrow road. It is found on the left 250 metres after leaving the village where it is possible to park 3 or 4 cars. NOTE: *Unfortunately there is no direct or defined access to the summit from above Cwm Cilio Farm. It is important to follow the description below to cross a short section of private land for which permission has been gained from the landowner.*

Walk up the road until just before the tarmac ends. Here a track branches off to the left. Follow this for 40 metres and go through the gate. There is a waymark on the gate post at the far side! DO NOT turn to the left as if going to Moel Bronmiod but continue straight ahead on the grassy track with a wall/fence to the right. After a short gentle rise the track levels somewhat to reach a gate. Pass through this. Follow the gently rising and still grassy track keeping the wall/fence to the right.

Garn Bentyrch, 228 metres is seen to the right. St Tudwal's Islands can also be seen to the right of Garn Bentyrch.

The track eventually shrinks and a path continues. Pass through a walled section to reach two gates some 100 metres apart.

Pass through the first of these to reach a ruin on the left. DO NOT go through the second gate but turn left through a gap in the wall by the ruin. Go through an old metal gate 10 metres beyond. Follow a faint path some 10 metres away from the wall on the right it to the top of the rise. The wall heads off downhill here. Instead of following it down contour across the hillside to where a short descent leads to a gate and the end of the access land. The next 250 metres are with permission of the landowner. PLEASE respect this and close the gate behind you.

Go through the gate and keeping above the marshy ground descend slightly leftwards to the obvious sheepfolds and a track below them. Turn right along this and through the gap in the wall into access land once more. Keep following the track to where it bends 90 degrees to the right and then goes left. At this point go to the right on a narrow path bearing slightly left and up to cross a tiny stream 5 metres before a wide gap in the wall.

Pass through this and continue straight ahead on a faint path which becomes boggy in parts. It bears right towards the wall and a gate. DO NOT go through this but go up to the left on the immediate right of a shallow trough on another faint path. At the path junction bear right and up to where it crosses the hillside diagonally up to the right to reach a low broken wall. Keeping this to the right continue up to pass through a gap between the wall and the fort wall. Bear up and left to reach the unmarked rocky and small summit. There is fine panorama from here.

Looking west the near peak is Moel Bronmiod 416 metres beyond which is Tre'r Ceiri 485 metres and Garn Ganol 564 metres, two of the peaks of Yr Eifl. To the left of these is the 'pimple' crowned form of Mynydd Carnguwch 359 metres and Garn Fadryn 371 metres. To the right of Moel Bronmiod 416 metres is Gyrn Ddu 522 metres, Gyrn Goch 492 metres and right again not far away is Bwlch Mawr 509 metres. Looking to the east is large form of Moel Hebog 782 metres. Left of Moel Hebog is Snowdon 1,085 metres. To the right the view takes in the Moelwynion and on the skyline the fine ridge of the Rhinogydd. The main obvious peaks in the Rhinogydd are left to right Rhinog Fawr 720 metres, Rhinog Fach 712 metres and Y Llethr 756 metres the highest mountain in the range. In the far distance Cadair Idris 893 metres can be seen.

To return to your car reverse the outward walk.

Walk 5
Traverse of the Eifl

Walk details

Height: *Tre'r Ceiri 485 metres, Grid Ref. SH 3743 4470*
               Garn Ganol 564 metres, Grid Ref. SH 3650 4474
               Garn Fôr 444 metres, Grid Ref. SH 3610 4572

Distance: *4¾ miles*

Time: *3½ hours*

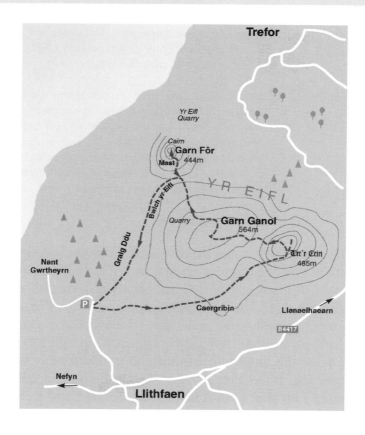

O.S. Maps:	1:25,000 *Explorer Sheet 254 or* 1:50,000 *Landranger Sheet 123*
Start:	*From the car park at the summit of the road from Llithfaen to Nant Gwrtheyrn Grid Ref. SH 3531 4399*
Access:	*Follow the B4417 to Llithfaen then follow signs towards Nant Gwrtheyrn*
Parking:	*Free*
Notes:	*Magnificent views throughout. There are several boulder fields that need care especially on Garn Ganol (Yr Eifl) and the ascent of Garn Fôr. There is a very short but awkward scramble just above the transmitting station to reach the summit of Garn Fôr. Be respectful of the hillfort on Tre'r Ceiri. It is, perhaps, the finest in the British Isles*
Going:	*Gentle paths lead to a steeper ascent through heather and rocks. The descent is also rocky and leads to a short boggy section. A rocky path leads to the summit of Garn Ganol. The descent is very rocky at the start and needs care. Easier going leads to Bwlch yr Eifl. A track leads up to the transmitter and a short scramble and rough steps lead to the summit. A very good track leads from Bwlch yr Eifl back to the car park*

This is a superb, must do walk with outstanding views from all three summits known as 'Yr Eifl'. These are: Tre'r Ceiri 485 metres, Garn Ganol 564 metres the highest hill on the Llŷn peninsula and Garn Fôr 444 metres. Initially the walk goes below Garn Ganol before ascending Tre'r Ceiri. The Iron Age hillfort is, perhaps, the largest in Britain and is remarkably well preserved. It is certainly one of the highest situated ones! From there Garn Ganol is ascended and finally

Garn Fôr. The return walk is along the obvious track back to the car park from Bwlch yr Eifl. Much more time can be spent just soaking up the fine views.

There is an information board at the car park and three pillars of granite. This is the memorial to the quarrymen who worked in the three western Yr Eifl quarries.

The three quarries are, Chwarel Cae'r Nant, Porth y Nant and Chwarel Carreg y Llam.

Cross the road from the car park to the finger post for the Coastal Path. (Ignore the track to the right starting from the wooden finger post.) Turn left along the track then right 50 metres further to go up a rougher track. Bear left at the 'Y' junction 30 metres further. At the next 'Y' junction go straight ahead. IGNORE the left hand track. Continue gradually up the wide path to reach a shallow grassy dip at another 'Y' junction. Follow the path on the right arm of the 'Y'. This soon crosses a very low broken wall and continues gradually up to where it veers right to a kissing-gate.

Pass through this and bear left climbing gradually to where conveniently placed stones in the marshy ground help to keep feet dry in wet weather. At the low

Garn Fôr

The Quarrymen's memorial at the car park below Yr Eifl

marker post continue straight ahead to pass through the next kissing-gate. Continue across some more damp ground heading towards Tre'r Ceiri to reach a low wooden post and path coming in from the right. The path starts to rise more steeply and near to what appears to be the summit pass through a 'gateway' in the substantial fort wall. Continue up past the old settlements to a 'Y' junction. Note this for the return walk. Follow the right arm and go up to the summit cairn.

There are outstanding views from here. Snowdon 1,085 metres and many mountains of Snowdonia are easily seen and to the southeast is Mynydd Carnguwch 359 metres.

The hillfort atop Tre'r Ceiri is, perhaps, the most spectacular in Britain and dates back to the Iron Age. It is situated at 450 metres some 35 metres lower than the actual summit. The name is believed to mean 'The home of Giants'. It is presumed to have been built around 200 BC. Most of the archaeological finds date around the period 150 to 400 AD placing it during the period of Roman occupation. Within the substantial walls are the remains of some 150 stone houses that could have housed around 400 people. The huts would have had turf roofs. It is also presumed that this was a summer settlement for shepherds who would also have houses much lower down during the winter. The water supply for the fort probably came from a spring outside the walled area.

There are two walls, an inner one embracing the main fort with a reinforcing outer wall on the west and northern sides. The inner wall has two main 'gateways' and three smaller ones. *The partial outer wall also has a 'gateway'.*

The earliest houses were stone roundhouses whilst later ones were rectangular. During an intermediate period it has been suggested that the houses were circular. Each were subdivided with internal stone walls creating two or three rooms.

Return to the noted 'Y' junction and turn right. Follow this path to another fort 'gateway'. Descend through this and continue down through the outer perimeter wall 'gateway' and turn right. Follow the path to the col and the start of the climb up Garn Ganol. Go up a boggy section to reach a stile over the fence. Cross this and continue quite steeply up over rough and sometimes boulder strewn ground to the summit. This is crowned with a trig point sporting a curious metal 4 with the letters A and H welded on. There is also a circular stone shelter.

Views again are outstanding. Beyond the closer Llŷn hills associated with Gyrn Ddu 522 metres and Gyrn Goch 592 metres the skyline comprises Snowdon 1,085 metres, Moel Hebog 782 metres the Moelwynion, the Rhinogydd and the Cadair Idris range. On clear days the Isle of Man, the Lake District and even the Wicklow Mountains in Ireland can be seen!

From the summit follow the path that starts off heading towards Tre'r Ceiri but overlooks Bwlch yr Eifl to the left. Pass a low, small cairn to where the path bears left and starts to descend. Boulders are reached and these are descended carefully gradually leftwards to reach easier walking on a clear path although it remains stony. Continue down to a path junction. This is level with three rock bluffs up to the left. Ignore the path going up to the left and continue down the smaller path to pass through two wood power line poles to a track on Bwlch yr Eifl. If you have had enough by now turn left along this back to the car park. To continue up Garn Fôr, cross straight over and up to a gate. Go through this although it is often left open and follow the track that bears right to reach a 'Y' junction. Continue up to two stone huts. Turn right at the right hand one and walk in front of it along a narrow path to a turning area. Bear left to the obvious steps leading up to the communication tower. Climb these to the enclosure. Turn right and walk around to the back of it until below a ruined stone hut. A few awkward steps up a slab, CARE, lead to stone steps at the left hand side of the hut. Climb these and bear left over a short section of rough ground to reach a very crude stone staircase. Follow this easily, thankfully on solid footing, through the boulder field to the summit ridge. Glorious views unfold as the summit is neared but much better ones are to be had from the top itself. The panorama is stupendous as with the other two peaks but with even closer views of the coastline.

Trefor owes its existence to the stone quarries on Yr Eifl, in particular on Garn Fôr, 444 metres, whilst the harbour was constructed for easy shipment. The granite like stone extracted from the huge quarry was used for kerb stones and 'setts' (small stone blocks or cobbles) in the cities of England and Wales. The rock is extremely hard wearing and is composed of porphyrite and quartz. Making 'setts' was a great skill that entailed a 3 years apprenticeship. Stone extracted from here was used to make the curling stones for the 2006 Winter Olympics in Turin. Wagons carried the stone down a cable controlled incline to the harbour. Samuel Holland started the quarry which prospered in the middle of the 19th century. At one time some 800 men worked in this quarry, the largest one of all in the area. Trefor was named after Trevor Jones, Holland's foreman.

Having soaked up the views return to the track, turn right and follow it back to the car park. There are great views of the Welsh Language centre at Nant Gwrtheyrn along the track.

Summit of Yr Eifl (Garn Ganol)

The wonderful and isolated village of Nant Gwrtheyrn, or properly Porth y Nant, was built during the second half of the 19th century to house the quarry workers of the booming stone industry. Before quarrying commenced in 1851 there were perhaps only three farms in the valley with 16 people living in seclusion. Twenty six new houses were built in 1878 to house the influx of quarry workers and the village thrived. When tarmac became the first choice for road building demand for stone marked the decline of the village. Stone quarrying was virtually abandoned mid-way during the Second World War. The villagers dispersed with the last people moving away in 1959. The cottages then started to fall into disrepair. In 1978 the whole village was in ruins but it was bought by a charitable trust, Ymddiriedolaeth Nant Gwrtheyrn who began restoring the houses and Nant is now the Welsh National Language Centre. Gwrtheyrn translates to Vortigern but 'King Vortigern' probably never visited here although he was in Snowdonia. There are many legends associated with village, 'The Three Curses', 'Rhys and Margaret', 'Elis Bach', 'The German Spy', 'The Eagle and the Baby', 'Luned Bengoch' and, perhaps, the most famous one of all, 'Rhys a Meinir'. All these and the story of 'Nant' can be found in an excellent book written by Dr Carl Clowes entitled Nant Gwrtheyrn *obtainable from the shop or café.*

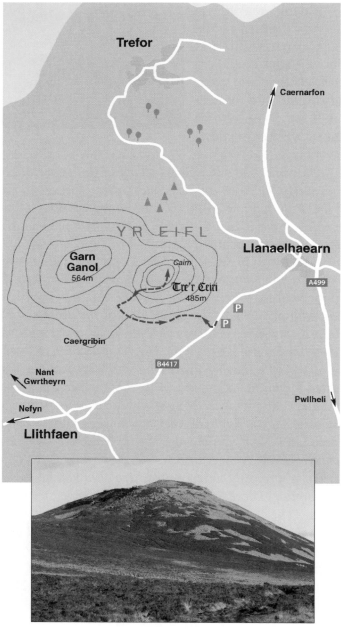

Tre'r Ceiri

Walk 6
Tre'r Ceiri

Walk details

Height:	*485 metres, Grid Ref. SH 3743 4470*
Distance:	*2¼ miles*
Time:	*1¼ hours*
O.S. Maps:	*1:25,000 Explorer Sheet 254 or* *1:50,000 Landranger Sheet 123*
Start:	*From a small rough layby by the side of the B4417* *between Llanaelhaearn and Llithfaen* *Grid Ref. SH 3687 4419* *If the rough car park is full there is a larger* *tarmacked layby at Grid Ref. SH 3801 4444. This is* *closer to Llanaelhaearn*
Access:	*Follow the B4417*
Parking:	*Free*
Notes:	*An easy walk but with a short ascent to the summit* *through heather and over rocks. Be respectful of the* *hillfort on the summit. It is, perhaps, the finest in* *the UK*
Going:	*Easily followed path there and back*

This is a very pleasant walk to a magnificent viewpoint and perhaps the best preserved Iron Age Hillfort in Britain, certainly one of the highest. It is suitable for those just wishing to see the fort or as an afternoon or evening stroll. The path is easily followed although it does become stony and rough towards the 485 metres high summit.

From the rough layby walk 100 metres towards Llithfaen to the obvious finger post up to the right. If walking from the larger layby head towards Llithfaen for 400 metres being mindful that this can be quite a busy road and CARE is needed. Turn right off the road up steps to the finger post indicating the way to Tre'r Ceiri. Continue up and go through the kissing-gate. Keeping the wall to the right continue up the grassy path to a gate.

Go through this and continue up the still grassy path and with the wall to the right passing through another gate or the gap in the wall to the left to a marker post. Continue up the grassy path as it veers left away from the wall. Pass by a long redundant stile following the narrower path up and across the hillside. Ignoring all turnings continue up past a 'paved' section when the gradient eases to reach a low wooden post. Turn right and go up to a short but steep section and pass through the narrow entrance of the outer wall into the fort.

Continue much more easily to the summit taking the right hand options at path junctions.

There are outstanding views from here. Snowdon 1,085 metres and many mountains of Snowdonia are easily seen and to the south east the obvious form of Mynydd Carnguwch 359 metres.

The hillfort atop Tre'r Ceiri is, perhaps, the most spectacular in Britain and dates back to Celtic times. It is situated at 450 metres some 35 metres lower than the actual summit. The name is believed to mean 'The home of

Giants'. It is presumed to have been built around 200 BC by the Ordovician tribe – the ancestors of the people of this part of Wales. Most of the archaeological finds date around the period 150 to 400 AD placing it during the period of Roman occupation. Within the substantial walls are the remains of some 150 stone houses that could have housed around 400 people. The huts would have had turf roofs. It is also presumed that this was a summer settlement for shepherds who would also have houses much lower down during the winter. The water supply for the fort probably came from a spring outside the walled area.

There are two walls, an inner one embracing the main fort with a reinforcing outer wall on the west and northern sides. The inner wall has two main 'gateways' and three smaller ones. The partial outer wall also has a 'gateway'.

The earliest houses were stone roundhouses whilst later ones were rectangular. During an intermediate period it has been suggested that the house were circular. Each were subdivided with internal stone walls creating two or three rooms.

Return to the layby by reversing the route of ascent.

Entrance on the southern side of
Tre'r Ceiri hillfort

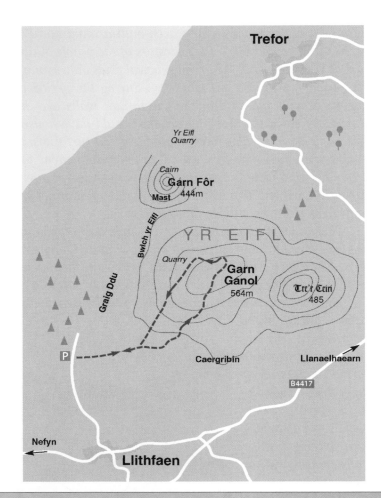

Yr Eifl
(Garn Ganol)

Walk 7
Garn Ganol (Yr Eifl)

Walk details

Height:	*564 metres, Grid Ref. SH 3650 4474*
Distance:	*2½ miles*
Time:	*1¾ hours*
O.S. Maps:	*1:25,000 Explorer Sheet 254 or* *1:50,000 Landranger Sheet 123*
Start:	*From the car park at the summit of the road from Llithfaen to Nant Gwrtheyrn* *Grid Ref. SH 3531 4399*
Access:	*Follow the B4417 to Llithfaen then follow signs to Nant Gwrtheyrn*
Parking:	*Free*
Notes:	*Magnificent views. Care needed on the rough rocky ascent and descent*
Going:	*Easily followed paths there and back but steep and rocky to gain the summit*

This is a great 2½ miles walk to the highest point on the Llŷn Peninsula at 564 metres and a magnificent viewpoint. Known generally as Yr Eifl its true name is Garn Ganol. A plethora of tracks at the start can be confusing but once established on the correct way the ascent is obvious. The path very gradually steepens and is a little rocky as the summit is approached. The walk can be done in 1¾ hours but allow 2 hours or more to appreciate the fine views. In August the hillside is awash with colour when the heather is in full bloom.

Start at the large car park with several bays on the left at the top of the hill from Llithfaen to Nant Gwrtheyrn. There is an information board here and three pillars of granite. This is the memorial to the quarrymen who worked in the three western Yr Eifl quarries. Grid Ref. SH 3531 4399.

The three quarries are, Chwarel Cae'r Nant, Porth y Nant and Chwarel Carreg y Llam.

Cross the road from the car park to the finger post for the Coastal Path. (Ignore the track to the right starting from the wooden finger post.) Turn left along the track then right 50 metres further to go up a rougher track. Bear left at the 'Y' junction 30 metres further. At the next 'Y' junction go straight ahead. IGNORE the left hand track. Continue gradually up the wide path to reach a shallow grassy dip at another 'Y' junction. Follow the path on the left and continue up to a wooden post.

Follow the path bearing up and left. (Ignore the path leading off to the right towards the rocky bluff.) Continue steeply on a path that cleverly avoids the majority of the boulder fields to the summit trig point and shelter.

There is a curious metal 4 on the trig point sporting the letters A and H! Views are outstanding. Beyond the closer Llŷn hills of Gyrn Ddu 522 metres and Gyrn Goch 492 metres the skyline comprises Snowdon 1,085 metres, Moel Hebog 782 metres, the Moelwynion, the Rhinogydd and the

Cadair Idris range. On clear days the Isle of Man, the Lake District and even the Wicklow Mountains in Ireland can be seen! There is a superb view of Trefor and the stone quarry of Garn Fôr 444 metres.

Trefor owes its existence to the stone quarries on Yr Eifl, in particular on Garn Fôr, 444 metres, whilst the harbour was constructed for easy shipment. The granite like stone extracted from the huge quarry was used for kerb stones and 'setts' (small stone blocks or cobbles) in the cities of England and Wales. The rock is extremely hard wearing and is composed of porphyrite and quartz. Making 'setts' was a great skill that entailed a 3 years apprenticeship to learn. Stone extracted from here was used to make the curling stones for the 2006 Winter Olympics in Turin. Wagons carried the stone down a cable controlled incline to the harbour. Samuel Holland started the quarry which prospered in the middle of the 19th century. At one time some 800 men worked in this quarry, the largest one of all in the area. Trefor was named after Trevor Jones, Holland's foreman.

From the summit follow the path that starts off heading towards Tre'r Ceiri 485 metres but overlooks Bwlch yr Eifl to the left. Pass a low, small cairn to where the path bears left and starts to descend. Boulders are reached and these are descended carefully and gradually leftwards to reach easier walking although it remains stony. Continue down to a path junction. Turn left where 3 rock bluffs are seen to the left. Go up to these and pass to the left of them and continue past curious mounds and walls of stone.

A faint narrow path continues on from this strange feature and descends gradually. After a very short rise bear right and continue the descent going out of the heather onto a more open hillside.

There is a great bird's eye view of Nant Gwrtheyrn along here.

The wonderful and isolated village of Nant Gwrtheyrn, or properly Porth y Nant, was built during the second half of the 19th century to house the quarry workers of the booming stone industry. Before quarrying commenced in 1851 there were perhaps only three farms in the valley with 16 people living in seclusion. Twenty six new houses were built in 1878 to house the influx of quarry workers and the village thrived. When tarmac became the first choice for road building demand for stone marked the decline of the village. Stone quarrying was virtually abandoned mid-way during the Second World War. The villagers dispersed with the last people moving away in 1959. The cottages then started to fall into disrepair. In 1978 the whole village was in ruins but it was bought by a charitable trust, Ymddiriedolaeth Nant Gwrtheyrn who began restoring the houses and Nant is now the Welsh National Language Centre. Gwrtheyrn translates to Vortigern but 'King Vortigern' probably never visited here although he was in Snowdonia. There are many legends associated with village, 'The Three Curses', 'Rhys and Margaret', 'Elis Bach', 'The German Spy', 'The Eagle and the Baby', 'Luned Bengoch' and, perhaps, the most famous one of all, 'Rhys a Meinir'. All these and the story of 'Nant' can be found in an excellent book written by Dr Carl Clowes entitled Nant Gwrtheyrn *obtainable from the shop or café.*

Keep going diagonally down and across the hillside on the now very faint path. This becomes much more pronounced as height is lost to join the track of the outward walk. Turn right along it back to the car park.

Walk 8
Mynydd Carnguwch

Walk details

Height: *359 metres, Grid Ref. SH 3745 4290*

Distance: *3½ miles*

Time: *2 hours*

O.S. Maps: *1:25,000 Explorer Sheet 254 or*
               1:50,000 Landranger Sheet 123

Start: *From the roadside parking on a quiet minor road*
               just off the B4417 close to Llithfaen
               Grid Ref. SH 3664 4328

Access: *Along the B4417*

Parking: *Free*

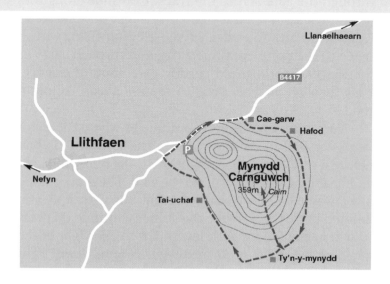

Notes:	*Great views*
Going:	*Easily followed roads and tracks but a pathless ascent*

This is a pleasant walk. It visits a wonderful viewpoint from this 359 metres high summit. Although ½ mile of the walk is on the busy B4417 it does not detract from it. Other than the ascent of the hill walking is either on roads or tracks.

Walk up the road to the B4417. Turn right down this for 700 metres to where there is a farm access track on the right. This is signed for Hafod and Tan-yr-Hafod. Turn right and follow the tarmac track for 450 metres to a 'Y' junction just before the farm. The tarmac track bears left whilst a rough track goes up to the right. Follow this up to where it levels. Continue to a gate. There is a small radio transmitting station to the left. Go through the gate across the track. Continue along the, more or less, level track to go through another gate. Keeping to the top edge of the sloping field, with a fence to the right, continue along and through a gap in the fence. A forlorn old rusting gate abuts the fence. Pass through another gate 50 metres ahead to join a road.

Turn right up this and continue to where there is a large flat pull in off the road on the left. This is just before a cattle grid. Turn right on to the grassy hillside and bear diagonally left up to the wall. The grassy slope gives way to a short stony section but with a clearly defined path. Once above the stones continue on grass to where the fading path levels. Up to the right is the large stony cairn of Bronze Age origin. Turn right

Mynydd Carnguwch

towards this, carefully climbing the loose rock to a much smaller cairn marking the actual summit and a shallow stone windbreak shelter.

There are superb views towards Yr Eifl with two visible Garn Ganol 564 metres the highest and to the right Tre'r Ceiri 485 metres, Gyrn Ddu 522 metres, Bwlch Mawr 509 metres, down to Llithfaen and across to the mountains of Snowdonia. Beyond the bay are the Rhinogydd. The fine form of Garn Fadryn 371 metres is easily seen to the south-west.

Having had enough of the view, descend back to the road. Turn right over the cattle grid and follow the road around to a cross roads. Turn right back to your car.

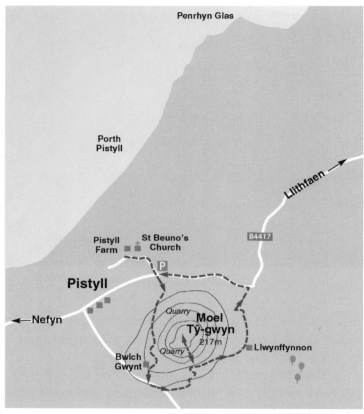

Pony on Moel Tŷ-gwyn

Walk 9
Moel Tŷ-gwyn

Walk details

Height:	*217 metres, Grid Ref. SH 3320 4166*
Distance:	*2¼ miles*
Time:	*1¼ hours*
O.S. Maps:	*1:25,000 Explorer Sheet 253 or* *1:50,000 Landranger Sheet 123*
Start:	*From the layby on the B4417 opposite the turning down to Pistyll church* *Grid Ref. SH 3308 4208*
Access:	*From the B4417*
Parking:	*Free*
Notes:	*Great views*
Going:	*There are intermittent paths across farmland and grassy slopes for ascending Moel Tŷ-gwyn. To visit Pistyll church it is easy road walking*

This is a pleasant circular walk that gives good views of the surrounding area. After the walk a visit to St Beuno's church in Pistyll is well worthwhile. This is easily done by driving down the dead-end road almost opposite the car parking layby to another small car parking area on the right a couple of hundred metres before the church.

From the layby walk towards Nefyn for 100 metres to a finger post and gate on the left. Go through the gate at the top of the steps and walk up the field bearing slightly to the left to reach a track and marker post. Go diagonally right across the field to a gap in a wall and a fence corner where this turns 90 degrees. Continue with the fence on the right passing through a gap between boulders. The path veers away from the fence to climb gently past ruins to where it climbs more steeply 50 metres to the left of small spoil heaps. Bear right and up above these, no path, to reach a stile and waymarker. Continue ahead as indicated on a narrow grassy path. Turn right through a gate with a waymarker above and left of the small quarry.

Keep the wall to the left and go down through a gate on the left 60 metres ahead. Climb over the stile 20 metres ahead and down some steps. Continue down to a marker post, steps and a gate. Go through this to join a track. Turn left along this to another gate with a finger post on the right. Pass through the gate to the minor road. Turn left along this. Turn left again, having passed a ruin on the right hand side of the road, 250 metres further where there is a finger post.

Follow the access track and go through a white gate. Walk through the gravelled courtyard and along a short section of walled track to a kissing-gate with a waymarker. Pass through the gate and bear diagonally left as indicated to a low, broken old wall and a marker post. Walk up the walled wide path to a gate. Go through this and ascend the slope ahead to the unmarked summit of Moel Tŷ-gwyn.

There are great views of Yr Eifl (The Rivals), Snowdon 1,085 metres, Moel Hebog 782 metres, the Moelwynion, Moel y Gest 263 metres above Porthmadog. On the far skyline is the fine ridgeline of the Rhinogydd. The Llŷn hills to the south west are Mynydd Nefyn 256 metres, Carreglefain 261 metres and Gwylwyr 237 metres. In the gap between Mynydd Nefyn and Carreglefain, Garn Boduan 279 metres is the hill rising above Nefyn.

Return to the gate but DO NOT go through. Turn left and keeping the wall to the right continue to a kissing-gate. Go through this and bear left with a low wall on the right and continue to go through a gap in the wall. There is a marker post here. Bear slightly left and down, low wall on the right, towards another kissing-gate seen in the distance. Pass through this and go down bearing left, SLIPPERY when wet. The path goes left at a post by the fence on the right and descends to a fence which is followed to a gate on the right by a farm, Llwynffynnon. Go through the gate and down steps to the farm access track. Turn left along it to the B4417 then left along this back to the layby and the end of the walk.

On Moel Tŷ-gwyn

From the layby drive down the dead-end road on the opposite side of the B4417 to the small car parking area on the right. Continue on foot to St Beuno's church.

The 12th century church at Pistyll is another one dedicated to St Beuno. It was used by Pilgrims on their way to Ynys Enlli (Bardsey). Three times a year the church is strewn with rushes and sweet smelling wild herbs. Rupert Davies, who played the French detective, Maigret, in the 1960's television series was buried here after his death in 1976. Nothing very much remains of the original church that was established by St Beuno in the 6th century other than a crumbling step by the old door and a corner stone, one of three known to exist, on the corner by the leper's window. The slate roof replaced the original thatched one some 120 years ago. The churchyard is oval in shape as was the custom all those years ago. Lepers came here hoping for a cure and were housed separately to the pilgrims in a hospice close by. The poor lepers had to stand outside whatever the weather and observed the service through the small windows. The tradition of celebrating the first Sunday in August, Lammas, has been revived by the parishioners here. Originally it celebrated the time when the first grain from the harvest was ground to bake a loaf. Prayers were offered for the remainder of the harvest to be safely reaped and gathered. Lammas derives from the Anglo Saxon word 'hlaef-mas' meaning loaf mass.

Walk 10
Moel Gwynus

Walk details

Height: *236 metres, Grid Ref. SH 3407 4229*

Distance: *2¼ miles*

Time: *1½ hours*

O.S. Maps: *1:25,000 Explorer Sheet 253 or*
                1:50,000 Landranger Sheet 123

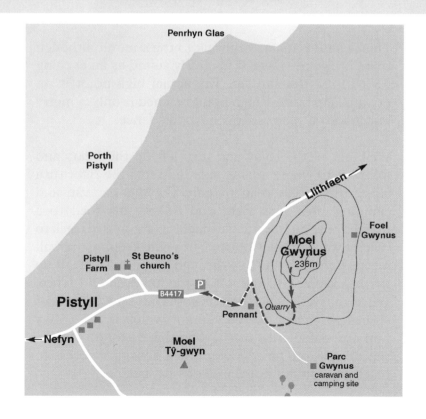

Start:	*From the large looping layby on the B4417 350 metres beyond the turning down to Pistyll Church when travelling towards Llithfaen from Pistyll Grid Ref. SH 3341 4211*
Access:	*From the B4417*
Parking:	*Free*
Notes:	*The true summit is on private land but the reachable high point only a few metres away is less than a metre lower and has the same views*
Going:	*There are intermittent paths across farmland and grassy slopes to reach the summit*

This is an unsatisfactory walk to the summit although there are good views. It is ideally suited as an evening walk to see the sun set. The actual high point is on private land but the high point reached is only .3 metre lower and 50 metres away beyond a fence.

Walk out of the layby and turn left up the B4417 and follow it to where a large sign indicates the right turn along the access road to Parc Gwynus caravan and camping site. Turn right and follow this road to a marker post on the left. Turn left up the grassy track to reach a wall corner. Continue to a gate keeping the wall on the right. DO NOT go through the gate. Turn left up the hill keeping to the left of the low wall and fence. When the wall ends continue with the fence to a pile of stones very close to the summit which is the grassy non accessible area just beyond the fence. (A gate on the right in the fence lower down does give access to reach the summit but this is private ground.)

The view from the summit area is good especially of Yr Eifl (The Rivals), Mynydd Carnguwch 359 metres, and Porth Dinllaen with Gwylyr 237 metres, Carreglefain 261 metres and Mynydd Nefyn 256 metres to the left of it. Beyond these is Garn Fadryn 371 metres whilst Mynydd Tirycwmwd 133 metres is to the right of St Tudwal's Islands. On the far eastern skyline is the ridge of the Rhinogydd.

Return to the layby by retracing your steps of the outward walk.

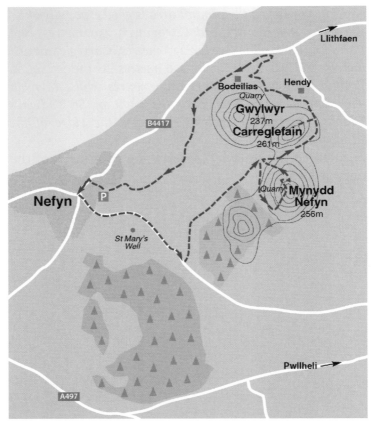

Looking down on the hamlet of Pistyll from Carreglefain

Mynydd Nefyn and Carreglefain

Walk details

Height:	*Mynydd Nefyn 256 metres, Grid Ref. SH 3249 4065* *Carreglefain 261 metres, Grid Ref. SH 3342 4109*
Distance:	*4½ miles for the full walk or 1¾ miles for the shorter walk*
Time:	*2¾ hours for the full walk or 1¼ hours for the shorter walk*
O.S. Maps:	*1:25,000 Explorer Sheet 253 or* *1:50,000 Landranger Sheet 123*
Start:	*From the Maritime Museum in Nefyn for the longer walk, Grid Ref. SH 3087 4064 or from a car parking area at the end of the road for the shorter walk, Grid Ref. SH 3205 4069*
Access:	*From either the Museum or minor road*
Parking:	*Free*
Notes:	*Great views, Care is needed on the summit of Carreglefain because there is a long vertical drop on one side*
Going:	*Grassy paths that sometimes become muddy predominate. There is a short but easy scramble to reach the summit of Carreglefain. The path below the spoil heaps to reach Nefyn is stony in places*

This is a grand walk. The views are especially good and wide ranging. In wet weather one short section of the walk is prone to be muddy. Care needs to be taken on the summit of Carreglefain as there is a long drop down the southern aspect. Carreglefain could be explained as 'echo mountain'!

Nefyn has a long history that dates back to 300 BC. The village is dominated by the hill overlooking the village, Garn Boduan 917 feet (280 metres). On the summit of this hill are the remains of an Iron Age hill fort with some 170 identifiable stone huts as well as the fort ramparts. The Romans were also here and recorded a tribe of people on the peninsula called the 'Gangani' who were also a tribe in Ireland. Nefyn possibly derives from the Irish/Gaelic Nevin or Cnaimhin. Nevin translates into 'Little Saint' whilst Nefyn is an alternative form of Nyfain who was an early Welsh female saint. In fact many old references use Nevin. The village could also have been named after Nefyn, one of the 24 daughters of Brychan, King of Madryn.

In 1284 Edward 1st held a tournament here to celebrate his invasion of Wales dedicating the festivities to King Arthur and the Knights of the Round Table. In 1355 the Black Prince, Edward the 1st's son, made Nefyn a royal borough remaining so until 1883. The Llŷn Maritime Museum is housed in St Mary's Church that was restored in 1825. Note the weather vane on top of the tower! There was a church here in the 6th century and it was an important staging point for the pilgrims heading to Ynys Enlli.

In the centre of Nefyn is St Mary's Well on Stryd y Ffynnon. It was rebuilt in 1868 and has a pyramid shaped roof above the well itself. Fishing, and in particular herring, played an important part of the town's economy in the 18th and 19th centuries. The coat of arms for the town incorporates three herrings.

From the Maritime Museum walk down to the B4417

and turn left. Follow the road through the village, passing St Mary's Well on the way, to the roundabout in the centre of the village. Turn left. Follow the road going slightly downhill between houses and along to a 'Y' junction. Take the left fork (right is a dead-end). Continue up the narrow and steep road to a left turn opposite a mirror on the right. Turn left. Continue along this until it ends, ignoring all turnings, to a car parking area on the right.

(*ALTERNATIVELY for the shorter version drive to here for a very pleasant afternoon or evening stroll.*)

Go through the kissing-gate straight ahead. Continue up the grassy track to where it steepens just before it becomes wide and lawn like! A rougher track goes off to the right from here. Turn right up this and follow it up to where it levels. Turn left on a faint path some 70 metres before a wall. Continue up between low gorse bushes. As height is gained the path becomes more obvious. A cairn is seen up to the right. Go up to this, the first of three tiny subsidiary summits. There is a lovely view of the lower lying land and the sea.

Continue over a lower summit to the main summit of Mynydd Nefyn. Facing out to sea drop down to the left and descend a vague grassy gully dotted with a few rocks to reach a vague track. Turn right to the obvious ruin. *The quarry face and the ruins are a part of a group of quarries collectively known as Foel Dywyrch.* Turn left down the track until a stone step stile is spotted over to the right 50 metres away. This is some 200 metres before reaching the wall seen ahead. Keep a look out for this as it is easy to miss!

Head over to and over the stile. Bear diagonally right up the path to where it levels. Continue past a small gate and stone step stile keeping the wall on the

Below Carreglefain

right to where a faint path turns left to climb Carreglefain. This path is 50 metres or so to the right of a scree slope composed of large stones. Keep to the right of the scree and continue up to a level area. Turn left and go across to a short, but easy, scramble to the summit from which there are superb views. They are similar to but slightly better than those from Mynydd Nefyn. CARE needed here as there is a high cliff face below.

The view, in a clockwise direction from the obvious finger like headland of Porth Dinllaen jutting out into the sea takes in Nefyn, Holyhead Mountain on the Anglesey skyline, Yr Eifl with their high point at Garn Ganol 564 metres, Snowdon 1,085 metres, Moel Hebog 782 metres, the Moelwynion and finally on the far skyline to the east beyond the bay are the Rhinogydd.

Return to the wall and turn left.

For the shorter version retrace steps to the wall and turn right instead of left. Go back past the gate and stone step stile following the obvious path as it veers right away from the wall to reach the stile crossed earlier. Continue down the track to the car parking area.

For the main walk continue along the path that gets progressively muddier in wet weather to arrive at the end of a track with a house to the right. There is a spring on the left. Follow the track down until just before a cattle grid turn left. Keeping the wall on the right continue to reach a crude stone step stile after a short walled section. Climb over the stile, carefully. Continue with the wall to the left into a short section of walled track. When this ends carry straight on to arrive at a cottage on the right at the end of a tarmac track coming up from below. Go down this and through a gate. Continue down and through another gate 50 metres before joining the B4417. Turn left down the road for 100 metres then turn left at the finger post for the Coastal Path and sign for Tŷ Mawr. Pass through a gate.

Turn up to the left 50 metres further at a marker post and walk up to and through a waymarked kissing-gate. The path continues and bears left at a 'Y' junction with a marker post. The next section is often muddy and continues to a waymarked gate. Go through this and continue slightly down past a marker post to a stone step stile and gate. There is a marker post and waymarker here. A grassy path continues across the lawn of a house, PLEASE respect their privacy, and go through a waymarked kissing-gate. A slightly overgrown path continues below the spoil heaps of the abandoned Gwylwyr Quarry seen up to the left. The path climbs up to a spoil heap and goes up steps and then down some to where the path becomes grassy. This ascends very gradually to two old gateposts. Descend to a track and continue down this to join a tarmac road at a finger post.

View of Yr Eifl from the lower slopes of Carreglefain

Gwylwyr Quarry was being worked in 1835 by Samuel Holland who had quarrying interests in the area as well as slate mines in Snowdonia. He combined the Eifl stone quarries with Gwylwyr to form the Welsh Granite Company. Between 1900 and 1904 Gwylwyr employed over 100 men. The quarry ceased production in 1937.

Turn left. Follow the track with a grassy middle up to where it levels. Continue along ignoring all turnings to a grassy bay on the left. Turn right here where there is a waymarker and follow the path past a waymarker on a gatepost. There is a fence to the right. Continue and pass through an old metal kissing-gate. Pass by Ffynnon John Morgan. Go through a kissing-gate on the right when the path ends. Turn left down the access track. When this bends to the left go straight ahead down a path, with a marker post on the right, and follow it down to a large grassy field in Nefyn. Keep to the right edge of this and pass through a kissing-gate at the far side. Follow the narrow alley to a finger post to arrive at the Maritime Museum which is well worth a visit.

Walk 12
Gwylwyr

Walk details

Height: *237 metres, Grid Ref. SH 3205 4125*

Distance: *2½ miles*

Time: *2 hours*

O.S. Maps: *1:25,000 Explorer Sheet 253 or*
                 1:50,000 Landranger Sheet 123

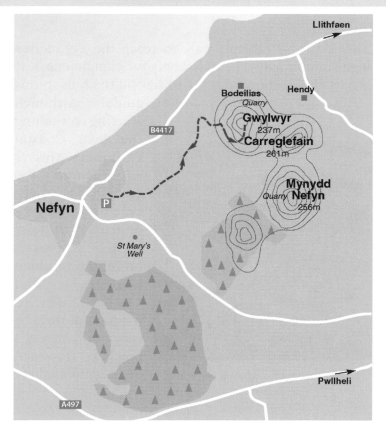

Start:	*From the Maritime Museum in Nefyn* *Grid Ref. SH 3087 4064*
Access:	*From the Museum*
Parking:	*Free*
Notes:	*This is more of a fight than a walk but is included for completeness. There are brambles and rocks in profusion. However, the views from the summit are superb*
Going:	*After leaving the Coastal Path the ascent is initially up a spoil heap before blundering up the brambles and rocks*

This is a very difficult walk to reach the 237 metres high summit and is included only for completeness. It is a 'walk' for those wanting to tick all the hills in this

Looking back towards Mynydd Nefyn from Gwylwyr

guide! Although starting off along the Llŷn Coastal Path once this is left behind the going becomes i n c r e a s i n g l y difficult with waist high gorse, brambles, hidden boulders and heather not to mention during the summer months bracken. However, once gained, there are superb views from the rocky summit by way of compensation!

Facing the museum go up the narrow alley on the left by the finger post. Go through a kissing-gate into a playing field and turn left. Keeping the hedge and stream to the left continue to a gravel footpath having a waymarker at the start at the other side of the stream. Follow this to where it starts to rise. Continue up to join a track. Turn left up this for 150 metres to a no entry sign. On the right is a finger post and kissing-gate. Go through the gate. Turn left and continue with a wall on the left.

Ffynnon John Morgan is seen to the right.

Continue up the gently rising path and pass through a gate. The path keeps on rising gently and zigs through a low wall to follow a fence on the left and a high hedge on the right. Continue to a track and turn left along it to reach a tarmac road after a slight descent.

Go down this to a finger post on the right and turn right. Follow the track to a gate. Pass through this and go straight ahead on a grassy path. At the marker post the path starts to descend and goes down gradually to reach some steps leading up to the base of a stony incline. Go up to the right and climb it to the drum house ruin at the top on the lower quarry floor.

Quarrying commenced in the 1830's and by 1835 it was owned by Samuel Holland. In 1844 he brought together several quarries in the area to form the Welsh Granite Company. After the granitic type of rock, a mix of porphyrite and quartz, had been blasted off, the setts were fashioned on the quarry floor. They were then lowered down the incline and across the Nefyn to Pistyll road by

Wern caravan site to a wooden jetty on the beach. Here they were loaded on to ships. In 1900 almost 100 men worked here but during World War I production more or less ceased. In 1920 production recommenced but on a much smaller scale before closing finally just before the onset of World War II. The jetty was then, unfortunately, blown up as a precaution against an enemy invasion.

Continue steeply up the continuation of the incline behind the drum house, on a hidden path, with more difficulty up looser stones and through gorse to arrive at the next level. There is a ruin of another drum house here. Turn right and head towards the wall turning up left alongside it. So far so good! The going now becomes dire. Hidden boulders, brambles and an ever increasing amount of gorse hinder walking. The least painful way I found was to follow the wall keeping it to the right until just before it levelled out and then turned up left and blundered through waist high gorse until just below the summit where a path revealed itself. Follow this leftwards to the rocky summit. There are fine views that make up for the toil.

Looking north is Yr Eifl (The Rivals), Snowdon 1,085 metres, Mynydd Carnguwch 359 metres, Moel Hebog 782 metres, the Moelwynion, Carreglefain 261 metres, Mynydd Nefyn 256 metres, Garn Boduan 279 metres and Garn Fadryn 371 metres. The view over Nefyn towards Porth Dinllaen is spectacular.

Having taken in the view and forgotten about the struggle to arrive here return to Nefyn by the way of ascent!

An easier way exists but involves climbing over two very high walls and moving out of access land!

Walk 13
Garn Boduan from Nefyn

Walk details

Height: *279 metres, Grid Ref. SH 3113 3936*

Distance: *2¼ miles*

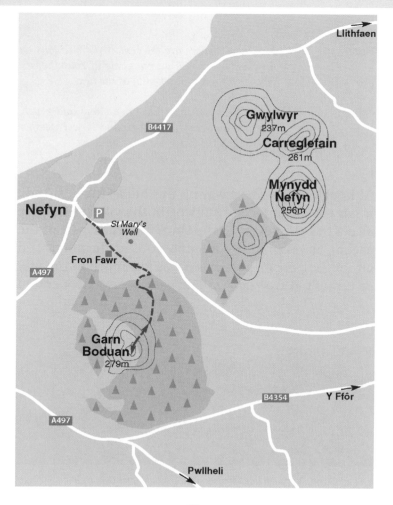

Time:	*1¾ hours*
O.S. Maps:	*1:25,000 Explorer Sheet 253 or* *1:50,000 Landranger Sheet 123*
Start:	*From the Parc y Ddôl car park in Nefyn* *Grid Ref. SH 3086 4040*
Access:	*From the car park and walking up the dead-end* *right branch of a minor road*
Parking:	*Free*
Notes:	*Fine views. There are the remains of a hillfort on* *the summit as well as remnants of roundhouses.* *Not as fine a way up the hill as the next walk*
Going:	*Easily followed paths but often stony and rough.* *There is an area of boggy ground in wet weather* *walking up the fields just after the start*

Although not as fine a way up this hill as the next walk it has the advantage of starting in the village. There is also a bus stop close to the start. The early part of the ascent is marred by recent conifer farming and although it opens up views it has left much in the way of unwanted tree debris. The path is also steeper and

Porth Dinllaen and summit wall of Garn Boduan

rockier than the other way described. However, once gained, the summit has the same wonderful views of the surrounding countryside.

The wall of the Iron Age hillfort on the summit of Garn Boduan

Walk out of the car park and turn left to a 'Y' junction. Walk up the right arm of the 'Y' which is signed as a dead-end road and named Y Fron. When the tarmac ends continue up the track to some derelict buildings and a junction of tracks. The main track bears right to a property. Turn off the main track and pass between derelict buildings. Turn left on the obvious path directly behind the right hand ruin and follow it up for 100 metres to a gate.

Pass through this and follow the sunken path into a field. Walk up this keeping the fence to the left to another gate. Go through this and walk up the field with the fence now to the right. The first few metres above the gate are extremely waterlogged in wet weather. Continue up to a kissing-gate.

Pass through this. Turn right. (The next bit to reach the track is all very scruffy with the remains of conifer farming.) Keeping the fence to the right continue to where the fence turns 90 degrees to the right. Turn left and follow the path up with a broken wall on the right to a marker post at the junction with a track. Go up the track straight ahead to where it levels and a marker post on the right. Turn right and follow the narrow steep path that becomes quite rocky as the top is neared to arrive on the summit and stone shelter.

There is a great view of all the surrounding hills including Yr Eifl which have Gwylwyr 237 metres, Carreglefain 261 metres and Mynydd Nefyn 256 metres in front of them. To the right of Yr Eifl is the unmistakeable form of Mynydd Carnguwch 359 metres with its summit cairn looking like a nipple! Beyond, the mountains of Snowdonia are clearly seen.

Return to the Parc y Ddôl car park by the way of ascent.

It is quite possible for the summit of Garn Boduan to have been the home of Buan. Boduan translates into English as 'the abode of Buan'. He was said to have been the grandson of the famous 6th century poet Llywarch Hen and places Buan around the years of 600 to 650 AD.

On the summit plateau there are the remains of a large Iron Age settlement. The first period of building took place around 300 BC. There are about 170 stone walled foundations of round houses with some being 8 metres in diameter and the circles are clearly visible.

Hillforts were the main settlement types during the Iron Age and later developments took place in pre-Roman and Roman periods before they were gradually abandoned in favour of dispersed upland settlements that were often small holdings and farmsteads. It is thought that these were only summer settlements. Evidence that animals were kept here has been found but no crop growing, hinting to the fact that the people who lived here did so occasionally preferring instead to live at lower altitudes. Perhaps, though, they were permanently occupied during the Roman invasion who used the area as a kind of 'holding' and confining area for the local population. (There is a Roman fort at Caernarfon and in those days was called Segontium.)

Walk 14
Garn Boduan

Walk details

Height: *279 metres, Grid Ref. SH 3113 3936*

Distance: *2 miles*

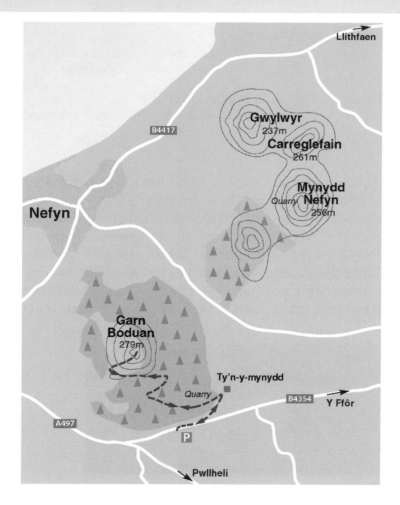

Time:	*1½ hours*
O.S. Maps:	*1:25,000 Explorer Sheet 253 or* *1:50,000 Landranger Sheet 123*
Start:	*From a large pull in on the side of the B4354 some* *400 metres beyond the turning off the A497* *Grid Ref. SH 3153 3874*
Access:	*Up the forest track*
Parking:	*Free, but don't block the forest access track*
Notes:	*Fine views. There are the remains of a hillfort on* *the summit as well as remnants of roundhouses*
Going:	*Easily followed tracks at the start. After leaving* *these the continuation path becomes stony and* *rough*

This is a pleasant walk to climb the hill starting from the south east side. There are superb views from the summit. Of the two routes described (the other one starts in Nefyn) this is much the better. There are lovely views during the ascent to the plateau immediately below the summit, the site of an ancient hillfort. Walking is mainly on forest roads but with the final part on a narrow and rough path that leads

Hut circles
on Garn
Boduan

through the southern wall of the fort. (The ascent from Nefyn is much steeper and is marred by a long section through an area that has been farmed for its conifers.)

Go through the kissing-gate to the right of the barrier and continue up the gradually rising track going around a left hand hairpin. Continue up to the track junction at the next hairpin. There is an information panel and marker post here. Turn left and go up the right hand track of two. Follow this gradually up to a track junction and a marker post. Ignore the right hand track and continue to where the track ends.

A narrow clearly defined path continues and rises gradually to where it levels.

The obvious hill slightly to the left is Garn Fadryn 371 metres. Turning round and looking back Moel y Gest 263 metres can be seen with the Rhinogydd forming the skyline beyond. Rising from the sea close to Llanbedrog, Mynydd Tirycwmwd 133 metres is also prominent.

Continue on the main path ignoring the right hand less clear path leading to a small 'roundhouse'. Pass several more remains of 'roundhouses', part of the settlement for the hillfort, towards the summit on a rougher path that splits just before the summit. Take the right hand clearer path to gain the wall guarding the summit from a small split rock on the left and lone dead tree up to the right. Clamber over the fallen stones and low wall to the summit. There is a stone shelter on top.

There is a great view of all the surrounding hills including Yr Eifl which have Gwylwyr 237 metres, Carreglefain 261 metres and Mynydd Nefyn 256 metres in front of them. To the right of Yr Eifl is the unmistakeable form of Mynydd Carnguwch 359 metres with its

Outer wall of hillfort

summit cairn looking like a nipple! Beyond, the mountains of Snowdonia are clearly seen.

Return to the car parking area by the way of ascent.

It is quite possible for the summit of Garn Boduan to have been the home of Buan. Boduan translates into English as 'the abode of Buan'. He was said to have been the grandson of the famous 6th century poet Llywarch Hen and places Buan around the years of 600 to 650 AD.

On the summit plateau there are the remains of a large Iron Age settlement. The first period of building took place around 300 BC. There are about 170 stone walled foundations of round houses with some being 8 metres in diameter and the circles are clearly visible.

Hillforts were the main settlement types during the Iron Age and later developments took place in pre-Roman and Roman periods before they were gradually abandoned in favour of dispersed upland settlements that were often small holdings and farmsteads. It is thought that these were only summer settlements. Evidence that animals were kept here has been found but no crop growing, hinting to the fact that the people who lived here did so occasionally preferring instead to live at lower altitudes. Perhaps, though, they were permanently occupied during the Roman invasion who used the area as a kind of 'holding' and confining area for the local population. (There is a Roman fort at Caernarfon and in those days was called Segontium.)

Garn Fadryn, Garn Bach and Moel Caerau

Walk details

Height: *Garn Fadryn 371 metres, Grid Ref. SH 2785 3517*
            Garn Bach 281 metres, Grid Ref. SH 2855 2937
            Moel Caerau 207 metres, Grid Ref. SH 2923 3548

Distance: *4¾ miles*

Time: *2¾ hours*

O.S. Maps: *1:25,000 Explorer Sheet 253 or*
            1:50,000 Landranger Sheet 123

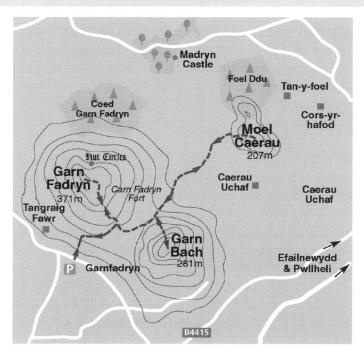

Start:	*In the village of Garnfadryn next to the old chapel Grid Ref. SH 2776 3453*
Access:	*Follow the A497 to Efailnewydd and turn on to the B4415. Follow this to Rhyd-y-cladfy. Turn right 2 miles beyond the village to Garnfadryn*
Parking:	*Free*
Notes:	*Superb views. Garn Fadryn has a rocky summit*
Going:	*Easily followed but steep path up Garn Fadryn, a pathless and short but steep grassy ascent of Garn Bach. Moel Caerau is reached and ascended by pathless grass and is set in the middle of a field*

This is a grand walk with terrific views. It takes in three summits and ascends Garn Fadryn first then Garn Bach and finally across the fields to to Moel Caerau. The summit of Garn Fadryn is rocky and has the feel of a much higher mountain. Moel Caerau on the other hand is a high point in a grassy field but with good views. Garn Bach is guarded by a steep but short climb to the fine cairn on the summit.

Walk back down the road from the layby past the chapel and turn left up the narrow track immediately beyond the house. Follow the track up with a grassy strip down the middle to where it bends right to 'Sweet Tamarind'. Go up the path straight ahead to a gate. Go through this and follow the path gently up to the right keeping the wall to the right.

When this starts to descend the path veers left and starts the long climb to the summit. A path zigs and zags up to a level area close to the summit. Cross this

Garn Fadryn, near to Garnfadryn hamlet

to reach a large cairn. Bear left then up to the rocky summit adorned with a trig pillar.

The view is extensive. To the south west is Mynydd Rhiw 304 metres and Ynys Enlli (Bardsey). To the north east are the obvious three summits of Yr Eifl (The Rivals). To the right of these is Snowdon 1,085 metres and right again is Moel Hebog 782 metres. On the very far eastern skyline are the Rhinogydd and even further away to the right of these it is possible to pick out Cadair Idris 893 metres. On really clear days the Wicklow Mountains in Ireland can be seen.

Return to the wall but 120 metres before reaching this turn left down a narrow path to the obvious stile. Climb over this with care as it is a bit rickety! Turn left and gradually veer away from the wall gradually descending across the field to a gate. Go through this and turn right. Follow the wall keeping to the left of it and climb over the ladder stile. Continue steeply still keeping the wall to the right to where it can be crossed and a path taken to the substantial cairn on the summit of Garn Bach for more good views.

Return back to and over the ladder stile and continue past the gate previously passed through. Continue keeping the wall on the left. Go easily over a low wall and bear right to reach the wall again. Keeping this to the left continue to where the path descends quite steeply into a hollow. On the left is a collapsed ladder stile but with stone steps set in the wall. Climb these to find that the other half of the ladder stile is intact! Turn right and keeping the wall to the right walk up the field to a fine stone step stile on the right. IGNORE the ladder stile straight ahead. Climb over the stone step stile and turn left through a gate. Follow the wall for 100 metres or so, keeping it to the left, then strike up the hill on the right to the grassy un-marked summit of Moel Caerau.

Return over the stone step stile and over the half ladder stile and stone steps to go up the steep climb. Continue to the gate before the next ladder stile and retrace steps to the stile at the bottom of the descent from Garn Fadryn. Climb over this and turn left back to the car parking area.

Garn Fadryn has an Iron Age hill fort on the summit and was possibly built in two stages. The first stage dates to around 300 BC, whilst the second stage reinforced the fort around about 100 BC. This enclosed some 26 acres. The third fort near the summit is believed to be 'The Castle of the Sons of Owain' (Gwynedd). He was the son of Gruffudd ap Cynan. It was mentioned as newly built in 1188.

Walk 16
Mynydd Cefnamwlch

Walk details

Height: *175 metres, Grid Ref. SH 2297 3390*

Distance: *2 miles*

Time: *1 hours*

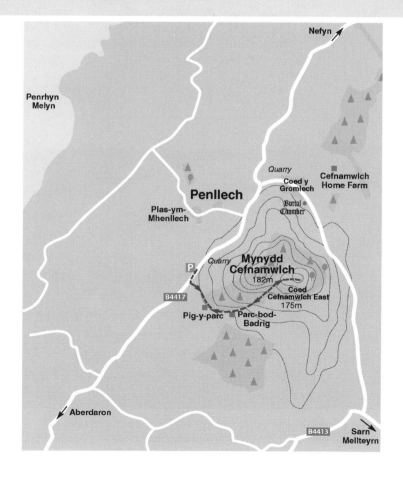

O.S. Maps:	*1:25,000 Explorer Sheet 253 or* *1:50,000 Landranger Sheet 123*
Start:	*At a small layby on the B4417 close to the track leading to Pig-y-parc* *Grid Ref. SH 2206 3392*
Access:	*Walk down the B4417 to the track and turn up to the left*
Parking:	*Free*
Notes:	*Good views. This walk ascends the East Peak. The West or Main Peak of 182 metres looks like it is an unremitting toil through dense brambles, high bracken and hidden boulders*
Going:	*Easily followed on a track and a grassy path*

The burial chamber on the northern side of Mynydd Cefnamwlch with Yr Eifl in the background

Although not reaching the main summit the east summit is still a worthwhile walk. There are lovely views of Tudweiliog and Ynys Enlli (*Bardsey*) and some of the Llŷn peninsula hills, Mynydd Anelog 192 metres, Yr Eifl (*The Rivals*), Garn Fadryn 371 metres, and Mynydd Rhiw 304 metres. The main summit looks like it is an unremitting toil through high bracken, brambles and stumbling over hidden boulders to reach it. It is not recommended to try.

From the layby walk down the road towards Aberdaron for 150 metres and turn left along the track. There is a finger post on the right. At the 'Y' junction go left and pass above Parc-bod-Badrig Farm. When the track bends to the right slightly turn left and walk up the grassy track to where trees on the right end at a track 'Y' junction. Turn right and go up the grassy path. At the next 'Y' junction go left and follow the track as it curves right up to the east summit from which there are good views. Retrace steps back to the layby.

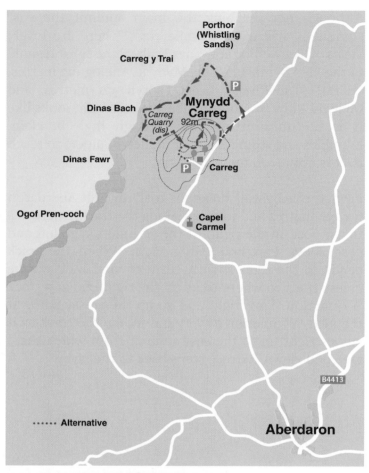

*The summit of
Mynydd Carreg*

Walk 17
Mynydd Carreg

Walk details

Height:	*92 metres, Grid Ref. SH 1637 2916*
Distance:	*1¾ miles for the main walk or ½ mile for the alternative*
Time:	*1 hour for the main walk or less than 30 minutes for the alternative*
O.S. Maps:	*1:25,000 Explorer Sheet 253 or* *1:50,000 Landranger Sheet 123*
Start:	*At the Whistling Sands National Trust car park* *Grid Ref. SH 1662 2951* *Alternative walk Grid Ref. SH 1628 2895*
Access:	*Walk out of car park on to the Coastal Path*
Parking:	*Fee payable at Porthor (Whistling Sands). Free parking for alternative walk*
Notes:	*Lovely coastal views. There is an old observation turret on the summit. There are picnic tables at the free site*
Going:	*Easily followed grassy paths on both walks*

This is quite an easy but very pleasant walk. There are lovely views from the old observation turret on the summit.

If so desired there is a café on the beach. It can be reached by turning left out of the car park and walking down the road for 400 metres. Porthor was called Whistling Sands by visitors because of the sound they make when feet are dragged over the drier and flatter parts of the beach. This sand, occurring on only two beaches in Europe has uniquely shaped particles that enable the 'whistle' to be made. Porthor, the original name, refers to the medieval Welsh commote of the region.

From the car park follow the path between the toilets to pass through a group of small trees before it opens out. Go past a 'viewing' seat that overlooks the lovely sandy beach of Porthor and continue past another. Turn left through a waymarked gate. Follow the grassy cliff top path with a fence to the left. Two small islands are seen down to the right. The first and smaller one is Dinas Bach. The other one beyond the small bay is Dinas Fawr. Continue to a waymarked kissing-gate. Go through this. On the immediate left is another. Turn left through it and continue up a fenced path to another kissing-gate. Go through this and turn left. Follow the track to the left to a small gate on the right of a wide opening in the fence!

Just beyond are the small Jasper quarries. These were mined in the 18th and 19th centuries. Jasper is a type of chalcedony being opaque and an impure variety of silica. The common colour is red. Other colours include yellow, brown and green. Breaking with a smooth flat surface Jasper is used for ornaments or as a semi-precious gemstone often highly polished.

Go through the gap and turn right. Keep the fence to the right and go up to a gate on the right at the top of the short rise. Turn left and initially follow the fence. When this swings right continue up to the turret and the fine viewpoint on the summit.

Views extend over Porthor and its whistling sands and northwards up the coast. The hills seen to the right from Porthor are, in a clockwise direction, Yr Eifl in the very far distance, Garn Fadryn 371 metres and looking south is Mynydd Anelog 192 metres. Across the bay of Aberdaron are the small islands of Ynys Gwylan-fawr and Ynys Gwylan-fach.

The turret on the summit was built during World War II as a lookout station. In those days it was probably topped with a glass dome sheltering the observers as they looked for enemy ships.

From the turret entrance go straight ahead then bear left passing below a small rocky subsidiary summit. Descend to a fence and turn left. Keep the fence to the right and follow it down. Where the fence turns 90 degrees to the right continue down alongside it quite steeply to a track and gate. Go through the gate and follow the track with the fence to the left at first to reach another gate. There is a National Trust sign for Carreg up to the right. Go through the gate to the minor road. Turn left down this to the left turn back to the National Trust car park.

ALTERNATIVELY there is a very easy walk to reach the summit and fine views. Do not turn down into the Whistling Sands car park but continue along the road past this turning for 600 metres. Turn right up a rough track immediately to the left of the farm buildings to the car parking area. If coming from the Aberdaron direction turn left immediately before the farm buildings at Carreg. Go through the kissing-gate at the top of the car park and bear right. Go easily up to and through another kissing-gate. Continue very gradually up to the turret on the summit. Retrace steps back to the car park. There are picnic tables here.

*Looking towards Mynydd Mawr and Ynys Enlli (Bardsey)
from Mynydd Anelog*

Walk 18
Mynydd Anelog

Walk details

Height:	*192 metres, Grid Ref. SH 1519 2721*
Distance:	*1¾ miles*
Time:	*A good hour*
O.S. Maps:	*1:25,000 Explorer Sheet 253 or* *1:50,000 Landranger Sheet 123*
Start:	*At the large rough car parking area by the phone box and chapel in Uwchmynydd* *Grid Ref. SH 1553 2634*
Access:	*Follow the minor road to Uwchmynydd from Aberdaron*
Parking:	*Free*
Notes:	*Spectacular views*
Going:	*Easily followed on roads, tracks or grassy paths*

This is a very good walk to gain one of the peninsula's finest viewpoints. However, it seems longer than it is! Although the walk is quite steep at the start the ascent to the summit is very rewarding. The views are spectacular from the summit and it is easy to linger. There are some lovely metal sculptures by the cottage on the way down.

From the car park bear right down the road for 10 metres and turn right into the dead-end road. Follow this up a rise to go through the waymarked gate. Follow the track leftwards up and across the hillside and through a gate. Keep following the track to where it goes up to the right in front of a white cottage to the fence and old style wall on the right. Continue up to and through a gate to a 'Y' junction 5 metres ahead. Bear right keeping to the left of the fence and go up to a post at a vague 'Y' junction. Bear left and pass above another white cottage, Craft View Cottage.

On the left almost at the end of the cottage is a narrow grassy path. This threads its way up the hillside weaving between stunted gorse bushes to the small summit cairn with extensive views.

Ynys Enlli (Bardsey) and Mynydd Mawr 151 metres are seen to the south as well as along the west coast of the peninsula all the way to Yr Eifl (The Rivals). Visible to the right of Garn Fadryn 371 metres is Snowdon 1,085 metres. The Wicklow Mountains in Ireland to the west are often seen. Cadair Idris, 893 metres is the obvious mountain mass in the very far distance beyond and right of Porth Neigwl (Hell's Mouth).

From the summit, having drunk in the great views, descend northwards on a grassy path

Craft View Cottage on the side of Mynydd Anelog

to where it levels. Turn right and follow the faint path to the wide green track below. Turn right along this until 25 metres before Craft View Cottage. Turn left and go down to a wall corner. Keeping the wall to the right continue down to a waymarked gate. Pass through this and bear left keeping to the right of the cottages at first then in front to another gate

Pass through this and turn left to follow a narrow grassy path to an upright stone and marker post. Continue ahead down a wider path. Where this ends go diagonally leftwards down the field to a kissing-gate. Go through this and bear right and up and through another kissing-gate. Continue ahead with the fence to the left and through a gate. Cross the track and pass through the kissing-gate. Follow the walled path ahead ignoring the kissing-gate on the left back to the car parking area.

The summit of Mynydd Anelog

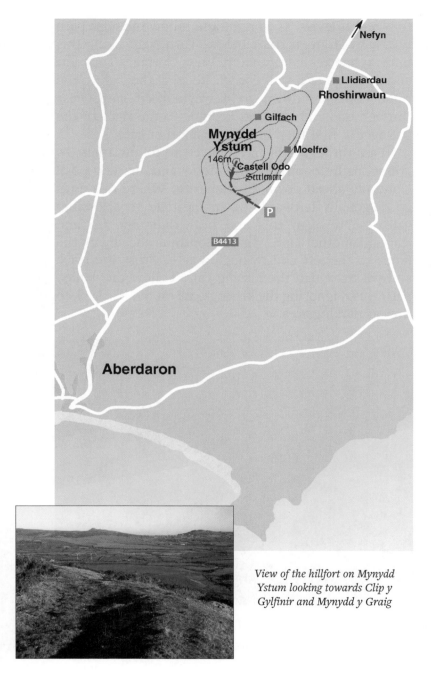

View of the hillfort on Mynydd Ystum looking towards Clip y Gylfinir and Mynydd y Graig

Walk 19
Mynydd Ystum

Walk details

Height:	*146 metres, Grid Ref. SH 1871 2848*
Distance:	*½ mile*
Time:	*30 minutes*
O.S. Maps:	*1:25,000 Explorer Sheet 253 or 1:50,000 Landranger Sheet 123*
Start:	*Roadside parking on a wide grass verge close to a track which is ¼ mile past Moelfre Farm on the Aberdaron side. NOTE the track is not marked on any of the OS maps! Grid Ref. SH 1884 2808*
Access:	*Follow the B4417 then the B4413 or from Aberdaron follow the B4413 where the track is found ¼ mile before Moelfre*
Parking:	*Free*
Notes:	*The start is not signed. Good views. The remains of an old hillfort are clearly seen on the summit and is known as Castell Odo*
Going:	*Easily followed up a track at the start then a pathless ascent to the summit*

This short linear walk visits a late Bronze Age/early Iron Age hillfort, Castell Odo. The ascent is reasonably steep and unfortunately no circular walk is possible.

View towards Mynydd Garreg from Mynydd Ystum

There are good views from the summit but little remains of the fort although the ditches are very easily spotted.

Walk up the track to where it splits at a 'Y' junction. Follow the right arm of the 'Y' and through a gate. Continue up the fenced track to go through another gate. Keep following the track up to where it bends right and ends at a level area. Continue across the field below the gorse bushes to where these end. Go up to the right of them to reach the trig point on the summit where the signs for the fort are still reasonably obvious.

Castell Odo, a late Bronze Age hillfort is one of the most important sites in Wales. Its origins date back possibly to the period of 800 – 600 BC. The fort has a diameter of 50 metres (165 feet) and has visible traces of eight circular huts. A legend associated with the site concerns a giant called Odo Gawr says he is buried under the pile of stones on the summit. Close by is a boulder known as Carreg Samson which was supposedly thrown by him from Uwchmynydd. Legend also says that there is a pot of gold beneath it and the holes in the boulder the imprint of his fingers!

Return the same way back to the road.

Walk 20
Mynydd Gwyddel and Mynydd Mawr

Walk details

Height:	*Mynydd Gwyddel 99 metres, Grid Ref. SH 1420 2519*
	Mynydd Mawr 151 metres, Grid Ref. SH 1403 2592
Distance:	*2 miles*
Time:	*2 hours*

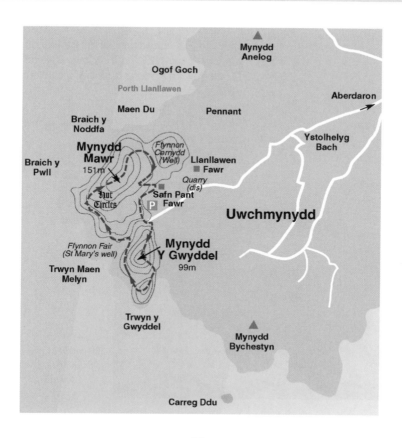

O.S. Maps:	1:25,000 *Explorer Sheet 253 or* 1:50,000 *Landranger Sheet 123*
Start:	*The large grassy car parking area at the end of the tarmac below Mynydd Mawr Grid Ref. SH 1422 2558*
Access:	*From Aberdaron follow the signs towards Uwchmynydd passing campsites to where the road becomes concrete*
Parking:	*Free*
Notes:	*Superb coastal views especially of Ynys Enlli. The descent to Ffynnon Fair (St Mary's Well) is only approachable at low tide and when the sea is calm. Difficult scrambling is required and is NOT recommended unless competent moving around on sharp, slippery rock. The path below Mynydd Gwyddel is narrow and crosses a steep slope where care is needed*
Going:	*Easily followed on grass and soil paths and signed for the Coastal Path*

Mynydd Mawr from Mynydd Gwyddel

This is a scenic walk with superb views. The views of Ynys Enlli (*Bardsey*) are amazing. Choughs are frequently seen on this walk. It is feasible for people who are adept at exposed scrambling to visit Ffynnon Fair (St Mary's Well). Mynydd Mawr is home to a very rare flower, the spotted rock rose, the only place in Britain where it is found.

Walk back down the road from the car park to the apex of the sweeping left hand bend and green path to the right going up Mynydd Gwyddel. There is a small caravan and camping site beyond the low wall and fence. Walk easily up the grassy path to the unmarked summit save for a few jagged rocks. There is a superb view of Ynys Enlli and across to the second summit of the walk, Mynydd Mawr.

Bear left from the summit and descend quite steeply to a marker post for the Coastal Path on a col.

Turn right. Pass another marker post and continue along the narrow path contouring around the steep slope passing several marker posts to a shallow, grassy valley and tiny stream. Cross the stream and contour left along to a marker post.

Looking back along the coastal path towards Ynys Enlli below Mynydd Gwyddel

An optional descent to Ffynnon Fair can be made from here if desired. However, this can only be recommended to people who are good rock scramblers. It is NOT recommended at all when it is high tide or when rough seas are running. Descend the path some 15 metres above the stream following the exposed path veering away from it. Scramble down intermittent, man-made, steps and easy angled rock to where it is possible to ascend a gently angled flake up to the right into an impressive alcove and the large deep pool. This pool of fresh water is often replaced by salt water at high tides but becomes fresh water again when the tide goes out! Return to the top of the steps and bear left up to the marker post. Just along the cliff top is the solitary Maen Melyn.

Ffynnon Fair is quite a strange place! Fresh water so close to the sea has led to some legends and customs. Here it is claimed that St Mary herself came across the sea and drank from the well. Reputedly an imprint of her hand and of her horse's hoof can be seen next to it! Fresh water is

Maen Melyn

replaced by sea water at high tides but is quickly replaced as the tide drops. It was one of the last places pilgrims stopped before reaching Aberdaron. One story about the well is as follows. At sunset a stranger told a beautiful local maiden that all of her wishes would come true if only she could carry the water in her cupped palms up the cliff and around Eglwys Fair (St Mary's Church) without spilling a drop! The church has now vanished but at one time it stood on the flat ground above the inlet.

Continue gently up to a slight col and another marker post. Turn right up to another then left to yet one more. At the next marker post turn right and ascend as indicated. Pass another marker post to the right of a small quarry. Continue up past the marker post to concrete bases and climb the concrete steps ahead to the lookout point on the summit of Mynydd Mawr. Follow the road back down to the car park.

As well as seeing Ynys Enlli across Swnt Enlli (Bardsey Sound), the Wicklow Mountains in Ireland are often visible and as well as the whole of Bae Ceredigion. South Stack lighthouse on Anglesey can be seen at night. The car park is the terminus of a road built during the Second World War to provide easy access to the former Coastguard lookout point. It was manned for 80 years or so before being 'retired' in 1990. Men were posted here during the Second World War to give early warning to Liverpool of imminent Luftwaffe air raids.

The headland of Braich y Pwll is the only known location in mainland Britain where the spotted rock rose is found. It has bright yellow petals with its characteristic spot at the base of its petals that only last a day! At various times of the year there is a profusion of wildlife and it is an ideal place to see choughs, peregrine falcons, kestrels, puffins, stonechats, guillemots and Manx shearwaters.

Dolphins, porpoises and seals can often be spotted in the sea. The chough is regarded as Llŷn's bird and a few circular symbols can still be seen in several places. Choughs have distinctive red legs and a red bill as well as being very black and glossy. A member of the crow family it is an acrobatic bird with a mewing cry confirming its identity. There are around 100 nesting pairs on the Llŷn due to the ideal breeding conditions, short grass, a rocky coastline, caves and a temperate climate. In Cornish legend King Arthur did not die at Camlan, his last battle. His soul migrated into the body of a chough with the red bill and legs were supposedly derived from the blood of that battle. It is said that it is unlucky to kill this bird.

Ynys Enlli is 1.9 miles offshore at this point. People have lived on the island since Neolithic times. During the 5th century it was a sanctuary for persecuted Christians. St Cadfan (who founded the church in Tywyn) came to the island in 516 and under his guidance St Mary's abbey was built. He was the first abbot on the island from 516 to 542. King Arthur reigned during this period. He had a sister called Gwenonwy whose name was given to Maen Gwenonwy, a rocky island at Porth Cadlan. She married Gwyndaf Hen (he is buried on Ynys Enlli) and they had a son called Hywyn who became the patron saint of the church at Aberdaron. For many centuries the Ynys Enlli was regarded as a land of indulgencies, absolution and pardon on the way to Heaven and the gateway to Paradise. It is rumoured that 20,000 Saints are buried on the island, however this can, possibly, be attributed to the fact that elderly monks retreated here near the end of their lives and possibly could be classed as such. Three pilgrimages to Ynys Enlli were the equivalent of one to Rome!

Walk 21
Mynydd Bychestyn (Pen y Cil)

Walk details

Height: *107 metres, Grid Ref. SH 1561 2430*

Distance: *3½ miles*

Time: *2 hours*

O.S. Maps: *1:25,000 Explorer Sheet 253 or
                   1:50,000 Landranger Sheet 123*

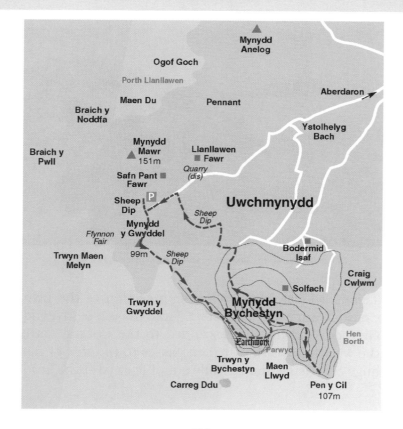

Start:	*The grassy car parking area at the end of the tarmac below Mynydd Mawr* *Grid Ref. SH 1422 2558*
Access:	*From Aberdaron follow the signs towards Uwchmynydd passing campsites to where the road becomes concrete*
Parking:	*Free*
Notes:	*Keep away from the poorly protected cliff at Parwyd*
Going:	*Easily followed paths on grass or on tracks and signed initially for the Coastal Path*

Ynys Enlli from the summit of Mynydd Bychestyn (Pen y Cil)

This is a lovely walk following a section of the Llŷn Coastal Path near to the start. From the top of Mynydd Gwyddel and having descended to the Coastal Path, the walk follows this. It then passes to the side of the huge cliff rising dramatically out of Parwyd at the head of an inlet before reaching the summit, named as Pen y Cil. The return walk to the car parking area crosses farmland.

Walk back down the road from the car park to the apex of the sweeping left hand bend and the obvious green path going up Mynydd Gwyddel 99 metres ahead. There is a small caravan and camping site beyond the low wall and fence. Walk easily up the grassy path to the unmarked summit save for a few jagged rocks.

There is a superb view of Ynys Enlli (Bardsey) from here.

Bear left from the summit and descend quite steeply to a marker post for the Coastal Path on a col. Turn left. Descend slightly and go through the gate. Bear right along the cliff top. Cross a footbridge and continue around to a waymarked gate. Pass through and continue gradually up the short rise with the fence to the left. Continue straight ahead below the small bluff when the fence bears left to reach a marker post. Gradually descend from this to a waymarked kissing-gate.

Go through this and follow the obvious path gradually up to a marker post. Another marker post is seen on the skyline at the top of a small knoll. Initially level, the path continues

Looking down the huge cliff of Parwyd

up to this post. Turn left and walk up to yet another marker post, again seen on the skyline. Pass this and continue to a fence and waymarker at the top of the huge 90 metres high cliff rising above Parwyd. Keep the fence to the right and passing a waymarker continue up to another fence. Turn left across the slope with the fence still to the right to the National Trust sign for Bychestyn. There is also an information panel here.

Go through the waymarked kissing-gate on the right and keeping the fence on the left continue to a finger post and waymarker in the corner of the field. Go through the gate straight ahead and continue to a waymarked kissing-gate up to the right 80 metres further. Pass through this to enter more National Trust land, Pen y Cil. Continue to the cairn on the summit of the headland.

Just before the summit cairn is a plaque dedicated to the National Trust who raised funds to buy the headland in 1970.

Return to the information panel and continue straight ahead keeping the fence to the right. Continue to a gate and go through this. There is another information panel to the right. Follow the track to a 'T' junction. Turn right and follow the narrow lane for some 300 metres to a junction with a track. There is a finger post on the right and pond to the right. Turn left and follow the track to a gate straight ahead, with a marker post on the right. Go through the gate and over the stile 50 metres ahead. Cross the field slightly leftwards to climb over another stile. Turn left and go through the gate 100 metres ahead to reach a track. Go left up this and follow it to the road then left along this to return to the car parking area.

Walk 22
Mynydd Cilan

Walk details

Height: *117 metres, Grid Ref. SH 2886 2421*

Distance: *6 miles*

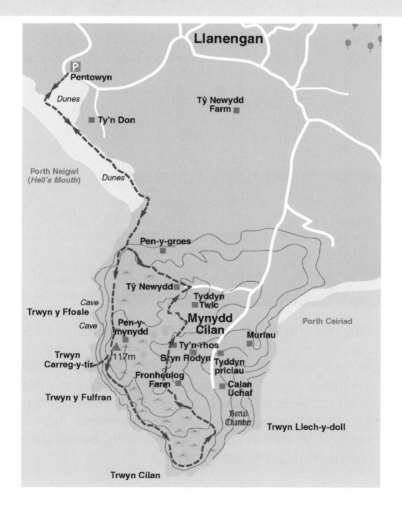

Time:	*3¾ hours*
O.S. Maps:	*1:25,000 Explorer Sheet 253 or* *1:50,000 Landranger Sheet 123*
Start:	*From the car park at Porth Neigwl* *Grid Ref. SH 2844 2666*
Access:	*Approach from Abersoch to Llanengan passing straight through the village to Porth Neigwl*
Parking:	*Free*
Notes:	*The grassy slope descended to view the rock strata ends in very steep slopes so care is needed and don't stray from the flat topped headland, it is long way down to the sea!*
Going:	*Easily followed on grassy paths or on tracks*

Approaching the summit of Mynydd Cilan

Some fine cliff scenery makes this a wonderful coastal walk. The paths are well signed and the tracks during the later stages of the walk, although not signed and appearing very complex, are in fact quite straightforward to follow. When surf is running high the sea at Porth Neigwl is very impressive indeed making it an ideal venue for surfers. Many can be seen waiting for that 'perfect wave'.

There are 4 miles of beach at Porth Neigwl. However, there are strong undertows and cross currents. In the last 180 years there have been 142 shipwrecks around the Llŷn coastline of which 30 have occurred in or very close to Porth Neigwl. It was a feared place by ancient mariners when returning home after a long voyage. Aptly named in English as Hell's Mouth it is exposed to the full force of any Atlantic storm having pushed its way between Ireland and Cornwall.

Interestingly Porth Neigwl refers to a certain Nigel de Loryng or perhaps Lohareyn. The Black Prince granted this area to him in recognition of his services in battles such as the Battle of Poitiers and Crecy during the wars in Gascony. Edward of Woodstock was born on 15th June 1330 and died on the 8th June 1376 and was the eldest son of Edward III. He was the first Duke of Cornwall becoming so in 1337 and then Prince of Wales in 1343. He was an exceptionally fine military leader. He was knighted in 1348. Edward died a year his father becoming the only Prince of Wales not to become King of England. His son, a minor, took the throne becoming Richard II when Edward III died.

The area around the car park at Porth Neigwl was once the site of a disputed bombing range in 1936 until 1945. Some of the remains can easily be seen. To the right of the path from the car park to the beach an oval narrow gauge rail track for propelling a model aircraft was used as a moving target by the trainee air gunners. The government had settled on this area for the range after the ones in Dorset and Northumberland were met with strong protests. The Prime Minister of the day, Stanley Baldwin, refused the Welsh appeal. Saunders Lewis wrote to the government stating that it was intent of turning 'essential homes of Welsh culture, idiom and literature into a place for promoting barbaric warfare'. In the 1935 Peace Ballot, 90% of Welsh votes were against aerial bombing and

Mynydd y Graig, Clip y Gylfinir and Mynydd Rhiw above Porth Neigwl (Hell's Mouth) at start of walk up Mynydd Cilan

there was nationwide opposition amongst MPs, local government and civic societies in Wales to the 'Bombing School' at Llŷn. On 8th September 1936 the bombing school building was set on fire by Saunders Lewis, Lewis Valentine and D. J. Williams. They immediately gave themselves up claiming responsibility. At the trial in Caernarfon a verdict could not be agreed and the 'Three' were sent for trial at the Old Bailey. Here they were sentenced to 9 months imprisonment and spent their time in Wormwood Scrubs. On release they were greeted as heroes by 15,000 people in Caernarfon. This act became known as 'Tân y Llŷn 1936' (Fire in Llŷn).

Mason Bees are a rare and solitary British bee that is found hereabouts. It builds its nest in the mud on eroding sand dune faces. As such Gwynedd County Council and National Resources Wales are trying to establish a suitable open habitat by managing the grazing levels to provide sufficient pollen for the bees.

Follow the path leading out of the car park towards the sea passing an information board to a finger post just before reaching the beach. Turn left. Follow the path with the fence on the left to a kissing-gate on the left. Go through this. Continue with the fence still on the left past a gate and finger post. Keep going straight ahead, staying with the fence on the left, past another gate and finger post. Pass to the left of a ruin. Go through the kissing-gate and continue ahead to where the path descends to the beach.

Turn left along this and cross a trickling stream OR, if the tide is favourable walk along the beach to this point. Not may hill walks start off like that! Go up to the left at a convenient point to the cliff top. NOTE that the point you climb up varies from time to time due to erosion. Continue along the top of the small mud cliffs and go over a waymarked stile. Walk up with the fence to the right and go through a kissing-gate. The path climbs up and across the hillside and passes through another kissing-gate. Walk across a short section of boardwalk then across the steep slope with the fence to the right to go through another kissing-gate. Pass through this. Cross 3 footbridges as the path goes below small cliffs. Pass 2 white topped posts and through another kissing-gate. Follow the narrow path straight ahead across the grassy slope to where it ascends, diagonally left, up to another white topped post where easier walking starts. Ascending very gradually cross the hillside to the next white topped post at the junction with a grassy track.

Turn right along this and follow it easily to a fence corner sporting a waymarker. Keep the fence to the left and continue gradually up to where the fence turns left at a waymarker. Continue ahead to a marker post at a 'Y' junction. Go up the right arm of the 'Y' and over to a marker post and the triangulation pillar on the summit of Mynydd Cilan. A prominent grassy headland is seen over to the right. Continue along the track from the summit for 150 metres to a grassy track leading down to the right towards Trwyn Carreg-y-tir.

The flat topped headland is a fine viewpoint to see the amazingly thin rock strata of Trwyn y Ffosle. The fine hill beyond it is Garn Fadryn. Care is needed here as the grass slope plunging down to the sea is extremely steep. The view towards Ynys Enlli (Bardsey) is superb.

Return to the track and turn right along it. After a slight descent and subsequent rise the lovely grassy track continues to a marker post and a vague 'Y' junction. The Coastal Path bears right and slightly down. Bear left and up very slightly to reach a track junction. Turn right. Follow the track around a 90 degree bend and continue up to reach a wall.

Turn left. Follow the track up with the wall to the right keeping any walls/hedges/fences to the right. Continue to a track junction. Go straight ahead to reach a wall. Keeping this to the right continue on the rough and in wet weather muddy track to reach an access track for the house on the right. Turn left up this and continue to reach a main track and other track junctions. Turn right along the main track and pass a house, Parc y Brenin to where the track bends 90 degrees to the right. Leave the track and walk straight ahead, ignoring tracks to left and right, on a grassy track to join another access track.

There is a small National Trust car park 120 metres away up the track to the right.

Turn left here and immediately left again to follow an access track to a small cottage on the left. Just before this turn left and walk around the cottage on its left on a good wide path. Bear left beyond the cottage to a prominent 'dogs must be kept on a lead at all times' sign. There is a reedy pond on the left. Continue gradually down the path/track with and old wall with fence on top to the right. When this turns right, note the old style construction, continue straight ahead to where the ground steepens quite suddenly. There is a track junction here. Go straight ahead easily down the steepening ground and bear left to a marker post for the Coastal Path. This was passed on the outward walk. Turn right and retrace steps back to the car park at Porth Neigwl.

Walk 23
Clip y Gylfinir and Mynydd Rhiw

Walk details

Height: *Clip y Gylfinir 270 metres, Grid Ref. SH 2239 2848*
             Mynydd Rhiw 304 metres, Grid Ref. SH 2285 2937

Distance: *2¾ miles*

Time: *1¾ hours*

O.S. Maps: *1:25,000 Explorer Sheet 253 or*
             1:50,000 Landranger Sheet 123

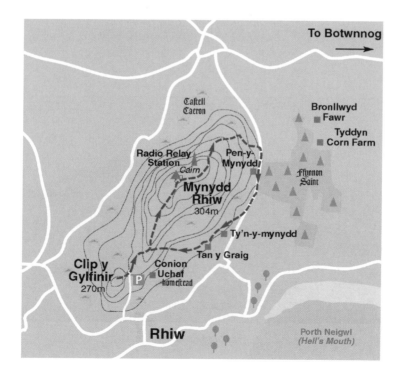

Start:	*From the parking area beyond the cattle grid close to the radar station*
	Grid Ref. SH 2250 2854
Access:	*From the cross roads in Rhiw turn up the road signed to Sarn. Go left at the 'T' junction and take the first right. Drive up the road until it ends and parking will be found*
Parking:	*Free*
Notes:	*Great views especially over Porth Neigwl (Hell's Mouth) towards Mynydd Cilan. The ascent of Clip y Gylfinir involves the use of hands on the very steep scramble leading up to its summit*
Going:	*Other than the steep rock and grass scramble on Clip y Gylfinir the walk follows tracks to reach the summit of Mynydd Rhiw then more tracks to reach a road which is followed back to the car parking area*

Mynydd Rhiw summit

The obvious and striking conical form of Clip y Gylfinir is well worth climbing before the ascent of Mynydd Rhiw. Not only does it give an outstanding view out towards Ynys Enlli (*Bardsey*), there is a superb view over the village of Rhiw and Mynydd y Graig. Looking east is the fine curve of Porth Neigwl (*Hell's Mouth*), with the Rhinogydd on the very far skyline. Although the summit of Mynydd Rhiw is somewhat marred by the communication tower it too is nevertheless a good viewpoint. This is a pleasant circular walk.

To ascend Clip y Gylfinir walk up the narrow access track towards the radar station and the striking form of Clip y Gylfinir. Turn right just after the left hand bend on an obvious path. This steepens considerably with height and is longer than it appears! A few steps using hands are needed close to the 270 metres high summit. The views are spectacular for such a small amount of effort, despite the proximity of the metalwork.

Return to the parking area to start the ascent of Mynydd Rhiw. Follow the obvious track straight ahead to a 'Y' junction close to the summit. Take the left arm of the 'Y'. Turn up to the left to reach the obvious trig point on the summit, after a very short but easy rocky scramble,. Having soaked up the views head off towards the enclosure surrounding the large communications tower. Pass to the right and in front of this following a track down to join a much more pronounced one. Turn left along this. Continue down to where, just beyond a small rocky knoll on the left, are the remains of a Neolithic stone axe 'factory' although nothing is really discernible amongst the gorse and heather! Keep following the track down to a narrow road.

The 'factory' dates back some 5,000 years to the Neolithic Age. The rock was suitable for making stone axes as well as other tools and was only discovered in 1958 during gorse burning activities. Hollows surrounded by low earth banks were composed of fine grained rock ideal for making stone tools. The preliminary excavation in 1958 revealed that the hollows were the silted remains of the quarry which is some 30 metres long and 6 metres wide.

Turn right along the road. In the wall on the left just after turning there is a gap beyond which is a stile.

Going over this there is a group of rocks from which there is a great view of Porth Neigwl (Hell's Mouth) and a good spot for a picnic.

Porth Neigwl is a favoured place for surfers but it was once a much feared area by sailors. Many wrecks are under the waves of this treacherous coastline. Once trapped in the mouth, there they were like flies in a Venus fly trap. Ships sank and crews perished. R. S. Thomas, a distinguished poet and former resident of Rhiw, wrote 'The Sea'; a section of which epitomises this:

> *'It has hard whips*
> *that it cracks, and knuckles*
> *to pummel you. It scrubs*
> *and scours: it chews rocks*
> *to sand: its embraces*
> *leave you without breath. Mostly*
> *it is a stomach, where bones,*
> *wrecks, continents are digested'*

Keep following the road and pass above Bryn Hyfryd, a house to the left. On the right 100 metres further on is a finger post, gate and stone step stile.

Pass through the gate or climb over the stile. *There*

is a fading sign for Ty'n y Mynydd on the wall. Follow the fenced track to where the fence on the left ends. Continue with the fence on the right to two gates straight ahead and one on the right. Pass through the right hand one. Follow the track, small length of fence to the right, going gradually up to reach a track coming up from the left. There is a pole here with several waymarkers. Go up the track to the right to a marker post at the junction with a track going left to right. Cross straight over and go up quite steeply on a path to climb over a stile spanning the wall and fence. There is a pole and waymarkers at the far side with a track just beyond. Turn left on this to join the track of the outward walk which is followed back to the car parking area.

Looking down on Botwnnog and across to Carneddol and Garn Saethon from Mynydd Rhiw

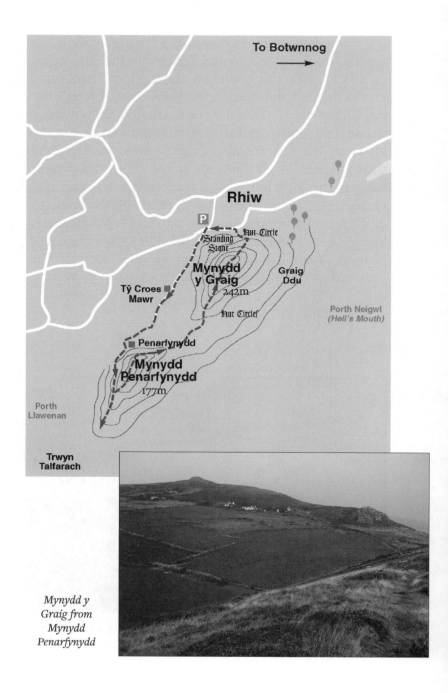

To Botwnnog

Rhiw

P

Hut Circle

Standing Stone

Mynydd y Graig
242m

Graig Ddu

Tŷ Croes Mawr

Hut Circle

Porth Neigwl
(Hell's Mouth)

Penarfynydd

Mynydd Penarfynydd
177m

Porth Llawenan

Trwyn Talfarach

Mynydd y Graig from Mynydd Penarfynydd

Walk 24
Mynydd Penarfynydd
and Mynydd y Graig

Walk details

Height: *Mynydd Penarfynydd 177 metres, Grid Ref. SH 2203
               2659*
               *Mynydd y Graig 242 metres, Grid Ref. SH 2281
               2744*

Distance: *3¼ miles*

Time: *2 hours*

O.S. Maps: *1:25,000 Explorer Sheet 253 or
               1:50,000 Landranger Sheet 123*

Start: *The cross roads in Rhiw
               Grid Ref. SH 2260 2775*

Access: *Follow the signed minor road from Aberdaron*

Parking: *Free*

Notes: *Wonderful views especially of Porth Neigwl (Hell's
               Mouth), Porth Ysgo and Maen Gwenonwy. Steep
               cliffs at Trwyn Talfarach and also at Mynydd y
               Graig*

Going: *Road at the start then grassy paths until almost the
               end of the walk where a short section of road back
               to your car*

This is a grand walk. The views from the seaward point
of Mynydd Penarfynydd, Trwyn Talfarach, are especially

fine. To the west there are dramatic views down to Porth Ysgo and Maen Gwenonwy, an island supposedly named after King Arthur's sister. To the east across Porth Neigwl (*Hell's Mouth*) and dominating the skyline is the serrated ridge of the Rhinogydd. The view from Mynydd y Graig is one of the best on the peninsula. There is limited road side parking in Rhiw. Please park so as not to obstruct the narrower sections of the road and avoid blocking driveways.

At the cross roads and with your back to the village turn left down the narrow road to a 'Y' junction. Follow the right arm of the 'Y' to where tarmac is replaced by gravel. Follow this track to where it is possible to turn left into the farmyard of Penarfynydd at a finger post and waymarker. Pass through the old and rusted metal gate above and to the left of the house. Turn right to the white topped marker post. Continue with the wall and fence to the right. Where these go downhill bear left to go up quite steeply.

There are increasingly spectacular views as height is gained, across to Porth Ysgo and Maen Gwenonwy to the west as well as the small islands of Ynys Gwylan-fawr and Ynys Gwylan-fach.

Continue past a marker post for 120 metres to a 'Y' junction. Take the right arm and continue to a small rocky summit on Trwyn Talfarach headland from which there are superb views, especially towards Aberdaron Bay to the right facing out to sea and across Porth Neigwl to Trwyn Cilan and the Rhinogydd in the very far distance to the left. Return to the marker post and bear up to the right to the broad ridge overlooking Porth Neigwl to the right. Turn left and continue easily to the summit of Mynydd Penarfynydd. There is a marker post next to the trig point. More great views are to be had from here.

Mynydd Rhiw 204 metres, with the communication tower, is directly ahead.

Bear right and continue gradually down the narrower ridge to a waymarked gate. Go through this and continue straight ahead descending easily and gradually to a marker post. Bear left here and go down to a kissing-gate where there is a National Trust sign for Penarfynydd. Pass through the gate to reach a walled grassy track. Follow this up and slightly to the left to go through a waymarked gate. Continue following the track to where there is large rock outcrop on the right. In front of this is a waymarked gate and stone step stile. This is easy to miss!

Climb over the stile and turn left. Turn right 50 metres further to go up a grass and gorse break to arrive at the left hand end of the small rocky tor. A better path is followed along the broad rounded ridge to the left. Pass through a short section of mid-calf height gorse to where the path rises gently across the right flank. Continue up to five metal posts. Between these is a small ruin. Keep following the broad ridge that ascends very gently to where the path steepens slightly. Pass easily through boulders to reach the unmarked summit of Mynydd y Graig.

The extensive view comprises Garn Fadryn

The village of Rhiw and Clip y Gylfinir from Mynydd Penarfynydd

371 metres, Yr Eifl (The Rivals), Snowdon 1,085 metres, Moel Hebog 782 metres and the Moelwynion. Beyond Cilan Head at the far side of Porth Neigwl and hugging the far horizon are the Rhinogydd and Cadair Idris 893 metres. Overlooking Aberdaron are the small islands of Ynys Gwylan-fawr and Ynys Gwylan-fach. Ynys Enlli (Bardsey) is easily spotted as is Mynydd Anelog 192 metres to the west.

Descend slightly then up to another summit of similar height. Keeping close to the edge on the left descend the path weaving between rocks to where a wall is een to abut against the cliff. Descend to this and climb easily over. There are the remains of a pole here. Vague intermittent paths descend diagonally rightwards to reach a waymarked gate. Go through this and follow the gravel track in to Rhiw and the minor road through the village to where your car is parked.

There are 3 small hill forts atop Mynydd y Graig along with hut circles and terraced fields dating back to the Iron Age (800 BC to 43 AD). Manganese was discovered in 1827 at Rhiw and the Benallt mine opened. Donkeys initially carried the ore to Porth Cadlan and Porth Neigwl. In 1914 an aerial ropeway was constructed passing over the village to a jetty at Porth Neigwl. During the Great War there was a great demand for manganese as it was utilised for strengthening steel. The mine became the major employer in the village. Some 200 people worked the mines and during the lifetime some 150,000 tons of ore were extracted. The mines closed after World War II. There were other mines in the area notably at Porth Ysgo (Nant Gadwen) where the ore was taken down to a jetty on the beach.

Walk 25
Foel Gron, Comin Mynytho and Foel Fawr

Walk details

Height:
Foel Gron 175 metres, Grid Ref. SH 3014 3108
Comin Mynytho 194 metres, Grid Ref. SH 2986 3189
Foel Fawr 190 metres, Grid Ref. SH 3055 3218

Distance:
2¾ miles

Time:
1¾ hours

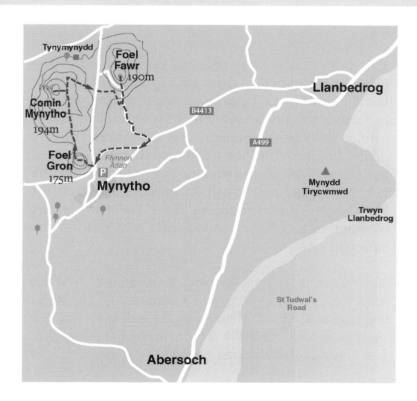

O.S. Maps:	1:25,000 *Explorer Sheet 253 or* 1:50,000 *Landranger Sheet 123*
Start:	*At the car park in Mynytho* *Grid Ref. SH 3022 3100*
Access:	*Follow the signed B4413 from Llanbedrog*
Parking:	*Free*
Notes:	*Good views. Comin Mynytho is painful to reach due to very dense gorse bushes and is, perhaps, best left to suffer alone. The summit of Foel Fawr has the base of an old windmill which is visible from afar*
Going:	*Clear paths and tracks with short sections of road walking*

This quite scenic walk takes in three summits. The pleasant ascent of Foel Gron, with good views from the summit, is followed by easy walking to a point where it is possible to gain the summit of Mynytho. This ascent cannot really be recommended as it is guarded by very dense, low gorse making walking quite painful as well as hiding hidden stones tripping you headlong onto the very prickly ground! It will only appeal to the ardent peak bagger! However, the ascent of Foel Fawr is very pleasant to reach the remains of a windmill on the summit.

The memorial hall in Mynytho is significant in Welsh history for the struggle to gain recognition for the Welsh language and culture. Mounted on the wall of the hall is a short poem which in Welsh is called an englyn. An 'englyn' is a traditional Welsh and Cornish short poem. It uses

The windmill base on Foel Fawr

quantitative metres which involves the counting of syllables and rigid patterns of rhyme and half rhyme. Each line contains a repeating pattern of consonants and accent known as cynghanedd.

The englyn by the poet R. Williams Parry is:
> Adeiladwyd gan dlodi, — nid cerrig
> > Ond cariad yw'r meini;
> > Cydernes yw'r coed arni,
> > Cyd-ddyheu a'i cododd hi.

In English this translates as:
> *It is built of poverty, not stones*
> *But love is its masonry,*
> *Shared aspirations are its timber,*
> *And shared commitment is what raised it up.*

Walk up the steps out of the car park to a 'Y' junction. Follow the right arm and continue up to the cairn and information panel on the summit.

There are great views over towards Abersoch, St Tudwal's islands and into Porth Neigwl (Hells' Mouth).

Continue over the summit bearing right and descend quite steeply to a pole at the junction with a track.

Cross straight over and keeping the wall to the right, continue gradually up to where the path levels and starts to go downhill beyond a power line. By turning left here it is possible to force an extremely prickly way to the summit of Comin Mynytho. Blunder/flounder up the heather and waist high gorse to the grass and rock summit only 250 metres away! Stumble back to where the path was forsaken.

Scratched and wondering why you did go to the summit continue much more sensibly with the wall to the right to reach a track. Turn right along this and follow it to a narrow minor road and finger post. Cross the road and turn right then immediately left over a stile by another finger post. Cross the field to the ruin. Turn right in front of this and head towards a power line. Go over a stile then bear left to yet another finger post by a stile. Cross this to join another minor road.

Turn left up this to where a National Trust sign indicates Foel Felin Wynt (the alternative name for Foel Fawr).

Go through a kissing-gate and follow the path to the left of the wall to the 'jam-pot' remains of the windmill and summit cairn.

The windmill was never successful due to the cross winds on the hill. Views extend from Pwllheli to Snowdonia.

Return to the road and turn left. Follow it down to the B4413. Turn right along this and walk through the village of Mynytho to return to the car park.

Walk 26
Mynydd Tirycwmwd

Walk details

Height: *133 metres, Grid Ref. 3290 3091*

Distance: *2¼ miles*

Time: *1½ hours*

O.S. Maps: *1:25,000 Explorer Sheet 253 or*
                    1:50,000 Landranger Sheet 123

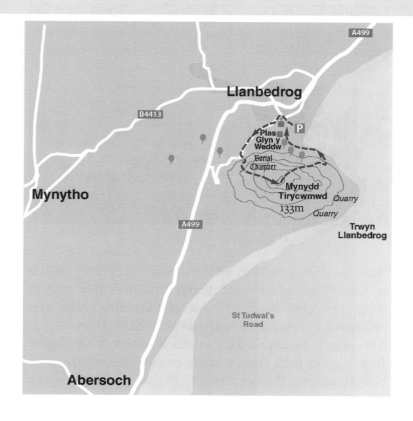

Start:	*At the National Trust car park in Llanbedrog Grid Ref. SH 3305 3148*
Access:	*Follow the A499 from Pwllheli or Abersoch*
Parking:	*Fee payable*
Notes:	*Superb views. The 'Iron Man' stands on top of a high cliff*
Going:	*Steep uphill and many steps after leaving Plas Glyn y Weddw, otherwise good paths followed by quiet road walking*

The Iron Man on Mynydd Tirycwmwd

This is a lovely walk to a fine viewpoint encompassing much of Cardigan Bay. At the famous 'iron man' on top of a high cliff there are spectacular views and the colourful beach huts on the beach make a fine sight. The return to Llanbedrog is much easier following at first a good path then a track before descending into the village and the car park.

Llanbedrog derives its name from the establishment of the church by St Pedrog in the 6th century. Note that for the village name the 'p' is mutated to 'b'! Legend tells us that Pedrog was a prince who gave up inheriting his father's kingdom and became a monk in Bodmin, Cornwall becoming one of the chief saints of Somerset, Devon and Cornwall as well as Brittany. He is also a patron saint of two other Welsh churches one in Pembrokeshire, St Petrox and another close to Cardigan at Ferwig.

The church suffered greatly at the hands of Cromwell's troops in the Civil War. The church walls were destroyed as were the ancient east window and several gravestones. Geoffrey Parry who led the army used the church to stable his horses. He was an ardent Puritan who, oddly, married the heiress of Wern Fawr in 1642. This family were staunch Royalists. They had a son called Love God Parry. In 1693 Love Parry, he rarely used his middle name, set about righting his father's wrongs to restore the church. The Love Parry family later established themselves at Madryn although they were all buried in the family vault at Llanbedrog.

The building of Plas Glyn y Weddw started in 1856 and completed in 1857 as a Dower house for Lady Elizabeth Love Jones-Parry of the Madryn Estate after the death of her husband in 1853. She had a large art collection and the house

The statue of 'Louise' at Plas Glyn y Weddw

was designed to house this collection by the architect Henry Kennedy. The cost of the building to include all the furniture, the fine gardens that included some quite exotic species of trees and plants as well as creating a network of paths through the Winllan was £20,000. Lady Love had intended to live in the house when Thomas, her son, married. He didn't do so until after his mother's death. In actuality she never spent a single night there although she was a frequent daytime visitor.

One of the reasons why the house was built there was that Lady Love's husband, Sir Love Jones-Parry was buried with his ancestors in the cemetery at Llanbedrog church which is very close to the house. Lady Love wanted to live near his grave and a special path was created to the churchyard. Another reason was that Elizabeth Caldecott, who became Elizabeth Jones-Parry following her marriage to the squire of Madryn, had been raised at the Cottage, a villa owned by the Madryn family near the church in Llanbedrog.

In 1896, Plas Glyn y Weddw came up for sale. Solomon Andrews, the wealthy Cardiff business man mentioned above, bought the house for £7,000. This gave him the golden opportunity to further his business developments along the peninsula. He turned the building into a public art gallery where he exhibited paintings by famous artists such as Gainsborough and Turner. Today there is a very fine tea room and the gallery still has exhibitions.

Walk out of the car park and turn left up the driveway to Plas Glyn y Weddw. Pass in front of the fine house noting the statuette of 'Louise' on the left. Continue up the tarmacked path above the car park and pass in front of the John Andrews open-air theatre into the wood. A gravel path continues rising gently at first to reach steps. Climb these more steeply to a finger post, seat and information panel. Turn left at the finger post along a more or less level path before descending gently a short distance to another finger post. A steep flight of steps goes up to the right, Climb these to their top where the path splits. Left here goes to the 'iron man' and spectacular views. CARE here as the sculpture is situated close to the cliff edge.

There have been three 'Iron Men' here. The original was constructed from wood. It was a figurehead from a ship and erected in 1919 on the headland by the family of Solomon Andrews (1835–1908) a wealthy Cardiff business man. He was also the owner of Plas Glyn y Weddw. Unhappily the wood figure was burnt by vandals and the villagers decided to erect another. Simon van de Put a local artist/sculptor who lived in Llanbedrog from 1976–1990 was contacted to see if he could construct a figure to replace the one burnt. It was constructed from recycled steel sheet and bar. This 'Iron Man' was erected in March 1980. Simon donated his time to the construction and only charged £50 for the materials used. Unfortunately, as the metal was untreated it quickly fell into decay and the man literally fell out of his boots! A refurbishment took place in 1987. This was paid for by a summer resident from Lytham St Anne's in Lancashire. When this finally fell apart a replacement was helicoptered into position over the Jubilee weekend on June 1st 2002. This new one was designed and built by local village talent. It included Berwyn Jones the designer and two craftsmen Davis and Hugh Jones. On a windy day the 'Iron Man' sings!

Return to the main path. Cross straight over ignoring the direction indicated for the Coastal Path. Continue directly ahead ascending steadily. Where the path opens out into heath the walking becomes easier. A wide grassy path continues ascending very gradually to the trig point some 50 metres away and 1 metre lower from the actual 133 metres summit.

There is a seat close to the trig point, as well as a cairn and toposcope. There is a superb view including St Tudwal's Islands and Abersoch, The main hills and mountains left to right are: Garn Boduan 279 metres, to the right of the windmill stump of Foel Fawr 190 metres, Gwylwyr 237 metres, Moel Gwynus 236 metres, Yr Eifl (The Rivals), Mynydd Carnguwch 359 metres, Gyrn Ddu 522 metres and Mynydd Cennin 262 metres. Crib y Ddysgl 1,065 metres, Snowdon 1,085 metres, Lliwedd 898 metres, Moel Hebog 782 metres, Moel Siabod 872 metres, Cnicht 689 metres, the Moelwynion and Moel y Gest 263 metres. Across the bay on the far eastern skyline are the Rhinogydd. The obvious ones are, from left to right, Moel Ysgyfarnogod 623 metres, Rhinog Fawr 720 metres, Rhinog Fach 712 metres looking like a tilted Table Mountain, Y Llethr 756 metres, Diffwys 750 metres and even as far down the coast as Cadair Idris 893 metres. To the west are Mynydd y Graig 242 metres and Mynydd Rhiw 304 metres. Behind the seat is Garn Fadryn 371 metres.

From the trig point head almost due west towards Llanbedrog on a grassy path descending very gradually to a track. Turn right down this to reach a tarmac road. Go down this to a junction. Bear right past campsite signs and follow the road down into the village ignoring all turnings. Turn right at the bottom of the hill to return to the car park.

Walk 27
Pen y Gaer

Walk details

Height: *80 metres, Grid Ref. SH 2986 2823*

Distance: *3½ miles*

Time: *1¾ hours*

O.S. Maps: *1:25,000 Explorer Sheet 253 or*
                 1:50,000 Landranger Sheet 123

Start: *At the car park between Abersoch School and*
                 Abersoch Hall
                 Grid Ref. SH 3121 2805

Access: *From Abersoch*

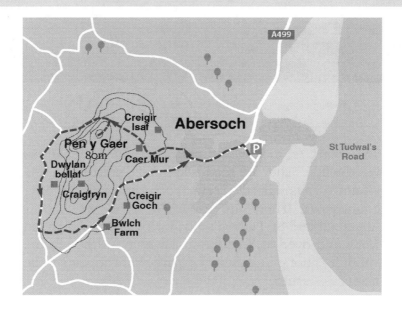

Parking:	*Fee payable (in summer)*
Notes:	*Muddy in parts during wet weather*
Going:	*Mainly roads and tracks with a descent down a muddy path*

View of Llangian from the lower slopes of Pen y Gaer, Abersoch

This walk is mainly on roads but is nevertheless worthwhile. The off road section is pretty and the summit has good views of the surrounding countryside. There are especially good views over Abersoch and St Tudwal's Road as well as to Mynydd Rhiw and over to Ynys Enlli (*Bardsey*). Although the summit is not on a public footpath there appears to be no access issues.

Walk out of the car park and turn right. At the 'T' junction, at the bottom of the slight hill, turn left. Walk up the minor road ignoring all turnings to arrive at a 'Y' junction. There is a post box and finger post here. Turn up the right arm of the 'Y' signed as a dead-end road. Keep following the road past the turning to Tan y Gaer until the tarmac ends at a 'Y' junction. Go up the right arm of the 'Y' through the gate signed for Bron y Gaer.

Follow the track past this large house to where the track bends to the right. Go through the kissing-gate on the left and follow a pretty track up to a marker post on the right. The path goes down to the right but before doing so turn left and follow the wall up keeping it to the left. At the top turn left through a gap in the fence to the unmarked summit.

The view east from here takes in Abersoch and St Tudwal's Road (an odd name for a bay). To the west the fine form of Mynydd Rhiw 304 metres is unmistakeable with its communication tower. To the left of this is Mynydd y Graig 242 metres. Mynydd Tirycwmwd 133 metres can be seen to the north-east. Above the village of Llangian is the village of Mynytho below the rounded form of Foel Gron 175 metres. The stunted windmill of Foel Fawr 179 metres can be seen to the right. Out to sea is Ynys Enlli (Bardsey).

Return to the marker post. Step down to the right and turn left. Keeping the low and very old wall on the left continue down. At a junction of paths go straight ahead and pass by a small, old quarry just before an old kissing-gate. Go through the gate and continue steeply down to a stile at the end of the low Bont Newydd. The last few metres can become flooded in wet weather with the ground quite boggy afterwards.

Climb over the stile to the road and turn left along it. Follow it for just over a third of mile to where a dead-end road leads off to the left. Turn left up this narrow road until the tarmac ends. Go through the kissing-gate on the right.

There are good views over Llanengan and the chimney above the village.

Llanengan is a pretty village with a good pub called The Sun. The parish church is supposed to be the prettiest on the Llŷn peninsula and is dedicated to Saint Einion Frenin. A church was established here in the late 5th or 6th century and was rebuilt around 1460 and extended in 1520. There is a link between this church and the monastery on Ynys Enlli. The ventilation chimney on the hillside above the village is all that remains of the Tanrallt lead mine. This closed at the end of the 19th century.

Continue along the path rising gently to go through a gate. Follow the track below the farmhouse and go through another gate. Bear right down the track to the road. Turn left up this and follow it all the way back into Abersoch passing the junction with the post box on the way.

Walk 28
Pen y Garn

Walk details

Height: *71 metres, Grid Ref. SH 3705 3535*

Distance: *1¼ miles*

Time: *45 minutes*

O.S. Maps: *1:25,000 Explorer Sheet 253 or*
                   1:50,000 Landranger Sheet 123

Start: *From the main car park in Pwllheli*

Access: *Pwllheli*

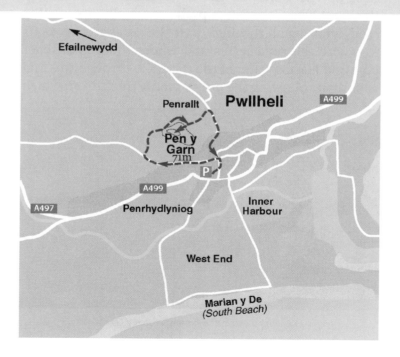

Parking:	*Fee payable*
Notes:	*Lovely view over Pwllheli*
Going:	*Road at the start then a grassy path/track with easy rock scrambling to gain the summit*

This is a very pleasant walk. There are great views from the summit of the Llŷn hills, Snowdonia as well as of Pwllheli. It is ideal as an evening walk or between rain showers.

Walk out of the car park to the roundabout having The Mitre pub at the far side. Cross the road and continue up Stryd Moch to the left of The Mitre. Go past the left turn up Ala Uchaf to the cross roads. Turn left up Penlôn Llŷn. Continue up the gradually steepening road, ignoring all turnings, past the derestriction signs to where the road levels and where there is a finger post and kissing-gate on the right. Go through this and bear right following the pretty grassy track, from which

Looking towards the summit of Pen y Garn

there is a great view of the summit, to where it ends at a ruin on the right. Continue on the grassy path for 10 metres and turn right.

Follow the narrow but clear path through bushes to reach open ground. With a fence to the right continue up to the base of the craggy base of the summit block. Scramble easily up this to the trig point.

The views from here are tremendous for such a lowly height and extend from the pointed form of Snowdon 1,065 metres to Moel Hebog 782 metres, Moelwynion, Rhinogydd, St Tudwal's Islands at Abersoch, Mynydd Tirycwmwd 133 metres above Llanbedrog and Garn Fadryn 371 metres as well as Yr Eifl.

From the trig point continue ahead towards the marina on a gradually descending path to reach a wall and fence. Turn left and keeping the wall to the right continue down to a 'T' junction of paths. Turn right and through a kissing-gate 10 metres further. Cross the top of the field to go through another kissing-gate. Continue along a short but pretty track and through one more kissing-gate, the far side of the larger gate to the left is inscribed Y Garn, to reach a narrow road. Turn right along this passing Coleg Meirion Dwyfor before descending the steep road back into Pwllheli.

Pwllheli is the major town on the peninsula. It was granted a charter in 1355 by Edward, the Black Prince (15 June 1330 – 8th June 1376), otherwise known as Edward of Woodstock. He was the eldest son of Edward III, a fine military leader, but never ruled as king, dying a year before his father. Edward's son came to the throne as a minor and became Richard II when Edward III died. A Wednesday market is held year round in the centre of the town. Shipbuilding and fishing were the predominant industries as well as a small stone quarry at Carreg yr Imbill (Gimlet

Rock), *but tourism has now taken over. The railway arrived in 1867. Plaid Cymru, the Welsh Parliamentary party, was founded here.*

During the 1890's Solomon Andrews (mentioned above) developed the town further. He built roads, houses and the promenade at West End as well as the tramway mentioned above.

Prior to World War II there was a holiday camp run by Butlins at Penychain. This was used as a naval camp during the war and was known as HMS Glendower. It operated a hospital just out of town at Bryn Beryl for the wounded and is now an NHS hospital. Once hostilities had ended Butlins once more took over the site returning it once again into a holiday camp. The camp has now been renamed Hafan y Môr.

Pwllheli marina and Cadair Idris on the far right skyline

Walk 29
Garn Bentyrch

Walk details

Height: *222 metres (low summit), Grid Ref. SH 4223 4189*

Distance: *1¼ miles*

Time: *1½ hours*

O.S. Maps: *1:25,000 Explorer Sheet 254 or*
               1:50,000 Landranger Sheet 123

Start: *Llangybi at the sign for Ffynnon Gybi at the side of*
               the road through village
               Grid Ref. SH 4267 4104

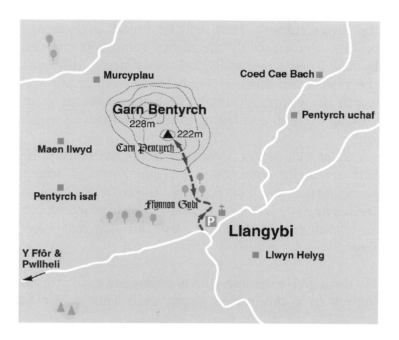

Access:	*A499 from Pwllheli to Y Ffôr. Continue past the cross roads in the centre of the village and turn right 450 metres further onto the road to Llangybi*
Parking:	*Free*
Notes:	*Great views. The true summit (228 metres) is on private land but the lower one with the trig point can be reached by a public path, DO NOT climb the walls to reach the true summit as they are high and loose. Passes by St Cybi's Well. It is muddy going up through the wood in wet weather. Iron Age hillfort on the summit*
Going:	*Grassy paths*

This is a splendid walk with much history attached. After visiting the wonderfully preserved Ffynnon Gybi (*St Cybi's Well*) the walk climbs up to the trig point on the lower summit. Here will be found an Iron Age hillfort. Unfortunately the higher summit is guarded by high loose stone walls and wire fencing. However, the views from this marginally lower summit are well worth the effort. Although the distance is not great visiting the well and taking in the views is well worth while.

Saint Cybi settled hereabouts in the 6th century. He was originally from Cornwall and travelled widely particularly in the Irish Sea area. During a dispute with Ireland he came here after landing on Anglesey whereupon he immediately struck a rock with his staff and water flowed!

Go through the kissing-gate and descend easily for 80 metres to a miserable-looking well. This is not St

Garn Bentyrch's lower summit

Cybi's. Pass through the kissing-gate on the right and continue straight ahead along the bottom edge of the field keeping a line of trees on the left. Continue to go through a 'gap' between upright stones. Follow the path with Afon Cybi on the left to an information board about the well on the left and a kissing-gate.

This is possibly the most elaborate well in this part of North Wales. It has been well known since mediaeval times for its healing properties. These were reported and extolled by the local vicar at that time by providing case notes. The water was said to heal the sick, lame and blind! William Price who owned the well was persuaded by the vicar to provide facilities for the pilgrims. This involved building cottages and providing beds.

When taking the cure it was deemed necessary to bathe several times a day. Between sessions pilgrims rested in a cottage and drank the water too. It was said that if you became warm whilst in bed the cure was working. All ailments were said to be cured including warts, tuberculosis, scurvy and rheumatism. Silver or pennies were thrown into the well by grateful patients.

A story relating to the well refers to the young local women. They used it to test the integrity of their loved ones. This was done by spreading their handkerchiefs on the water. If they floated south it was a good sign but definitely not if they went north.

Go through the kissing-gate and follow the path down to the ruin. The well is very impressive and the outflow goes down to the right of the old pavement to a latrine. Above and behind the ruin on the left is a waymarked gate. Go through this and follow the path slanting quite steeply up to the left. In spring many bluebells scent the air. In wet weather this path can become very slippery. The path levels and goes through another waymarked gate. Pass through this and turn right. Continue up the hill bearing slightly

Ffynnon Gybi

right to a marker post by a broken low wall going right to left.

Cross the wall and bear slightly right going up to the top right hand corner of the field to a marker post and gate. Pass through this and continue with increasingly good views keeping the wall on the right and through another gate with marker post. Continue, still with the wall to the right, to the fort close to the trig point on the lower summit. There are superb views from here.

Beyond the wall Moel Hebog 782 metres is seen with Snowdon 1,085 metres visible to the left it, Moelwynion; Moel y Gest 263 metres rising above Porthmadog and the skyline ridge of the Rhinogydd. To the right is Mynydd Tirycwmwd 133 metres rising whale like from the sea, Garn Fadryn 371 metres and the isolated from of Moelypenmaen 153 metres rising above a sea of flat fields. To the right of this is Garn Boduan 279 metres, Mynydd Nefyn 256 metres and Carreglefain 261 metres. Beyond the trig point are the hills of Yr Eifl (The Rivals). In front of these is the unmistakeable form of Mynydd Carnguwch 359 metres.

The hillfort, also known as Carn Pentyrch, has an innermost ring with a thick, high stone wall. This, though, is possibly mediaeval. The other two easily seen lines consist of walls and banks and are, most likely, to be prehistoric.

The main summit is 200 metres away to the north-west and is 6 metres higher. There is no right of access to this and it is guarded by high loose stone walls and fencing. Return by retracing steps as for the ascent back to the well and the road.

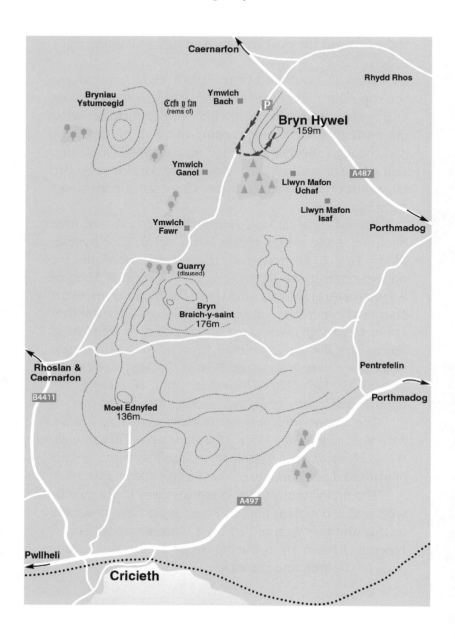

Caernarfon

Rhydd Rhos

Bryniau
Ystumcegid

Cefn y fan
(rems of)

Ymwlch
Bach

Bryn Hywel
159m

A487

Ymwlch
Ganol

Llwyn Mafon
Uchaf

Llwyn Mafon
Isaf

Porthmadog

Ymwlch
Fawr

Quarry
(disused)

Bryn
Braich-y-saint
176m

Rhoslan &
Caernarfon

Pentrefelin

B4411

Porthmadog

Moel Ednyfed
136m

A497

Pwllheli

Cricieth

Walk 30
Bryn Hywel

Walk details

Height:	*167 metres, Grid Ref. SH 5151 4177*
Distance:	*1 mile*
Time:	*45 minutes*
O.S. Maps:	*1:25,000 Explorer Sheet 254 or* *1:50,000 Landranger Sheet 123*
Start:	*From a layby next to a gate on the very minor road* *leading up from the A487* *Grid Ref. SH 5129 4185*
Access:	*Follow the A487 to the turning*
Parking:	*Free*
Notes:	*Great view of Moel Hebog. Footpaths seldom walked and somewhat overgrown*
Going:	*Boggy just after the start then up the field*

The walk to the summit is somewhat unsatisfactory. Footpaths in the area have not been used for years and have become overgrown. This is the most practical way of ascending this hill. The view of Moel Hebog 782 metres is, however, is spectacular.

Walk up the road from the layby, away from the A487, to a house on the right. Opposite this is their car parking area. On the left of this is a hurdle stile. There is the remains of an old finger post here. Climb over the stile and turn right and down. Swampy ground is quickly encountered to reach a footbridge over the tiny stream. Cross this and then find a way through the entanglement to a stile. This section is easier than it first appears.

Climb over the stile into more swampy ground. Follow this up to where the ground is firm and bear left to reach the summit. This, like Mynydd Ednyfed, has curious boulders on the summit.

The view of Moel Hebog with Moel yr Ogof 655 metres and Moel Lefn 638 metres to the left is a fine one indeed. To the left of Moel Lefn is the Nantlle Ridge group of hills. From left to right these are Cwm Silyn 734 metres, Mynydd Talymignedd 653 metres, Trum y Ddysgl 709 metres and Mynydd Drws-y-coed 695 metres. The fine looking hill rising above Porthmadog is Moel y Gest 263 metres.

Retrace steps back to the layby.

Cricieth town from its castle

Cricieth beach and castle

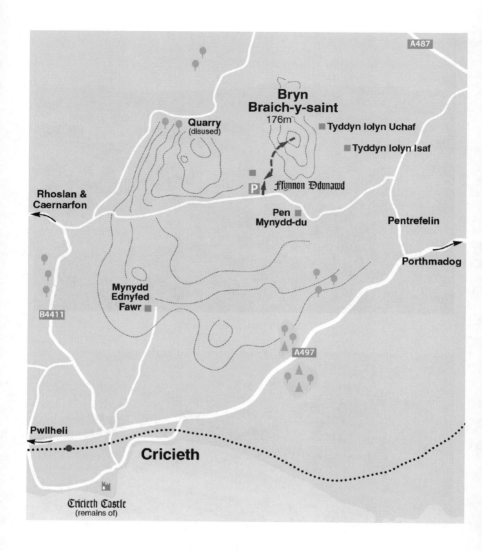

Walk 31
Bryn Braich-y-Saint

Walk details

Height:	*176 metres, Grid Ref. SH 5143 4052*
Distance:	*¾ mile*
Time:	*30 minutes*
O.S. Maps:	*1:25,000 Explorer Sheet 254 or 1:50,000 Landranger Sheet 123*
Start:	*At the junction with the access road to Braich-y-Saint Farm Grid Ref. SH 5121 4008*
Access:	*Follow the A487 to the turning*
Parking:	*Free*
Notes:	*Good views from the summit. Infrequently walked*
Going:	*Track and then across grassy slopes to summit*

Like others in the area this is not a very satisfying walk. Footpaths on the hill have not been walked for years but the summit does have good views.

Walk down the access road towards the farm. Opposite the first farm building there is a stile to the right of a gate. Climb over this – carefully. Turn right along the track and through the next gate. The track now bends to the left. Go straight up the hill in front keeping the wall to the right to reach a track. Cross straight over and go up the grassy slope to the summit. This too has boulders adorning the summit. The views are very similar to Bryn Hywel.

The view of Moel Hebog 782 metres with Moel yr Ogof 655 metres and Moel Lefn 638 metres to the left is a fine one indeed. To the left of Moel Lefn is the Nantlle Ridge group of hills. From left to right these are Cwm Silyn 734 metres, Mynydd Talymignedd 653 metres, Trum y Ddysgl 709 metres and Mynydd Drws-y-coed 695 metres. The fine looking hill rising above Porthmadog is Moel y Gest 263 metres. The Rhinogydd form the skyline beyond Moel y Gest. Cricieth castle can also be seen.

Return the same way back to your car.

*Summit view from Bryn Hywel looking towards
Moel yr Ogof and Moel Hebog*

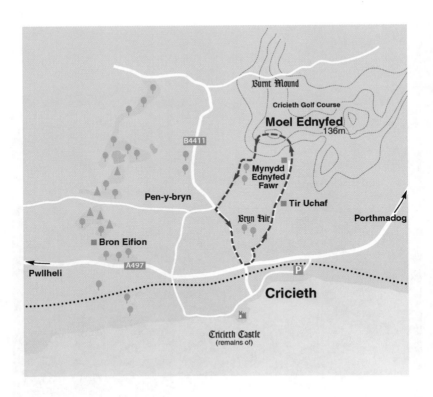

Walk 32
Moel Ednyfed

Walk details

Height:	*136 metres, Grid Ref. SH 5023 3938*
Distance:	*2 miles*
Time:	*1½ hours*
O.S. Maps:	*1:25,000 Explorer Sheet 254 or 1:50,000 Landranger Sheet 123*
Start:	*Roadside parking in Cricieth Grid Ref. SH 4992 3828*
Access:	*Turn off the A497 in the centre of Cricieth on to the B4411 and park on the roadside just up the hill where possible*
Parking:	*Free*
Notes:	*Good view over Cricieth from the summit. Paths on the OS map are confusing. Access is via the golf club road NOT as marked on the map up Nant y Wyddan*
Going:	*Road and grassy paths. In wet weather the paths beyond Mynydd Ednyfed country house are very boggy in wet weather*

Although this is a good viewpoint the walk to the summit is a little unsatisfactory. Paths shown on the OS map to avoid a road walk at the start are now completely overgrown, the stiles have collapsed and the paths seem not to have been walked for many years. Nevertheless it is worth doing solely for the views from the summit or after a bad spell of weather. NOTE: mid-way through the walk the path visits the golf course so it is important to stay on the path and be mindful of rogue balls.

Return to the road junction with the A487 and turn left. Opposite the Prince of Wales pub turn left up the minor road and walk past the Billiard Hall. Keep following the road up to reach the golf club car park. From the far end of this follow the track that bears right at first then a path goes up to the left to go through a very old kissing-gate. This is awkward to pass around! Once this has been negotiated bear left up to the summit. This has a curious boulder on top having a large but old staple drilled into it. There are also other boulders forming a rough circle.

There is a fine view of Cricieth castle from here.

Descend almost due west from the summit and cross a low wall heading for a wall which is followed on its left to the obvious kissing-gate in the right hand side of the field. Go through the gate and follow the short length of fenced and walled path to the access road for Mynydd Ednyfed, a fine country house providing luxury group accommodation.

Turn right as indicated by the finger post and follow the road for 100 metres to another finger post. Turn left as indicated through the kissing-gate. Keeping close to the wall, with a fence on top, on the left continue to a waymarked kissing-gate. Go through this and bear slightly right across the field to a waymarked gate mid-way along the wall in front. Go through this and follow the sunken wide track/path to another gate. *All this section from leaving the road is very muddy and swampy in wet weather.* Go through this to an access road.

Follow this to the B4411 and an almost hidden finger post. Turn left along the path alongside the road back to where your car is parked.

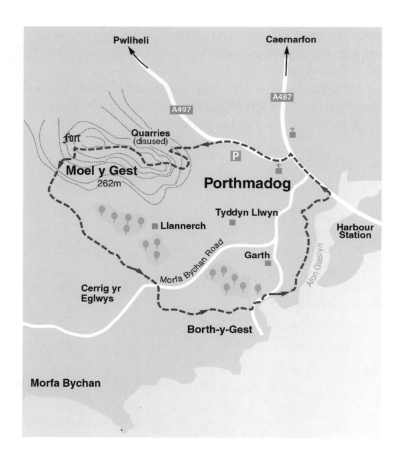

Walk 33
Moel y Gest

Walk details

Height: *262 metres, Grid Ref. SH 5495 3894*

Distance: *4½ miles*

Time: *3 hours*

O.S. Maps: *1:25,000 Explorer Sheet 254 or*
                1:50,000 Landranger Sheet 123

Start: *Small layby by the side of the A497 in Porthmadog almost opposite the petrol and caravan centre Grid Ref. SH 5622 3892*

Access: *From Porthmadog*

Parking: *Free*

Notes: *Superb views. The hill feels much bigger than it is. Care is needed on the very steep start to the descent*

Going: *Steep and rocky paths until after the steep descent then grassy. Road walk from Borth y Gest into Porthmadog*

This is a wonderful walk. Although it is not classed as a mountain Moel y Gest really does feels like one and far higher than the modest 263 metres summit suggests. The ascent is very well worthwhile, although it is steep with some rocky bits. Having gained the summit the views are spectacular on a clear day. The Glaslyn and Dwyryd Estuaries are prominent with the fine Rhinogydd towering behind and Snowdon 1,085 metres is very clearly seen along with Moel Hebog 782 metres and the Nantlle Ridge to the left of it. Beyond Porthmadog are the Moelwynion, the higher left hand one is Moelwyn Mawr 770 metres and the lower Moelwyn Bach 710 metres are clearly seen. Initially the descent from the summit is steep and rocky and needs care to discover the correct line. Once found the path is fairly obvious to reach easy walking for the return to Porthmadog via the pretty Borth y Gest.

Porthmadog is now a lively town with some great shops and cafes. Between 1807 –1811 William Madocks built his Cob across Afon Glaslyn to drain Traeth Mawr for agricultural use. It was then that Porthmadog started to develop. This 1 mile long 'embankment' allowed the river to scour out a new natural harbour and the first wharves were built in 1825 allowing small ocean going ships to dock there. Slate was carted down from Blaenau Ffestiniog to Afon Dwyryd then shipped to Porthmadog. As the demand for slate increased so did the size of Porthmadog. The tramway from Blaenau was created in 1836. In 1873 some 116,000 tons of slate from the quarries was shipped out. Over a thousand ships used the port every year. Ship building commenced and three-mast schooners, known as Western Ocean Yachts, were built. The last one was built was in 1913. Other industries evolved such as foundries, timber saw mills, slate works, a flour mill, a soda pop plant and a gasworks were constructed.

A wide path leaves the pull in at a finger post signed for Moel y Gest. Follow the wide path upwards through the wood, the ground being covered in bluebells in spring, to a 'Y' junction. Follow the narrower right arm of the 'Y' ignoring the much more obvious left arm.

Continue up and pass through a gap in a low wall to another 'Y' junction. Again follow the right arm of the 'Y' and walk quite steeply up to a junction of paths. There is a three trunked birch tree here and often a marker stone. A path continues ahead. DO NOT follow this. Instead zig acutely left. Continue gradually up to the low point between tree bedecked and rocky summits and a 'Y' junction.

Turn steeply up to the right to where the rocky path emerges from the wood.

There are great views from here over Porthmadog, the Glaslyn/Dwyryd Estuary behind which is the Rhinogydd range of mountains. To the left are the Moelwynion and the fine conical shape of Cnicht 689 metres, nicknamed the Welsh Matterhorn!

The path eases briefly and passes through a low broken wall where the path becomes steep again. As height is gained Moel Hebog rising above Tremadog and the Nantlle Ridge come into view. Continue steeply to a sudden levelling. There is a wonderful view of Morfa Bychan and Cricieth from close to the low wall.

Bear right and keeping the wall to the left follow it up then down towards the col between the summits east and the higher west summit. Just before the col the path veers to the right away from the wall and follows a broad but rocky easy angled ridge. Turn right at the 'Y' junction below frowning rocks and descend slightly to a path junction. Bear left. At the next 'Y' junction follow the left arm and go gently up, as the trig point comes into view over to the left, to a short rocky descent. Continue across to the next 'Y' junction and go up to the left to the trig point and marvellous views. The actual summit some 1.5 m higher than the trig point is 20 metres south.

Snowdon 1,085 is easily seen along with Moel Hebog 782 metres, the Nantlle Ridge, the Moelwynion and across the estuary the Rhinogydd dominate the skyline. There are also great views along the coast towards Cricieth and the Llŷn peninsula. To the south is the fine sweep of the Cardigan Bay coastline.

The initial very steep descent goes down the seaward side of the hill starting some 20 metres away from the trig point. It is difficult to locate but once found it is easy to follow. The path twists and turns avoiding the more rocky bits as it descends to turn right towards a hurdle stile. Go over this onto a much clearer and gentler path down grass that keeps to the right of a wall as it descends. After a short steeper and rocky section the path bears right then zigs left to descend to a tall, old and rusted iron gate. Go through this, great view over to Cricieth. Walk diagonally leftwards to the gap in the wall at the bottom left hand corner of the field.

Go through the gap and turn immediately left over the stone step stile sporting a marker post. Follow the path between low walls straight ahead to go through a waymarked gate. The path bears slightly left and continues down to join a track. Turn left along this and through a gate. Follow the track to a stile to the left of wide gates. Climb over the stile to the Porthmadog to Morfa Bychan road.

There is a finger post here indicating the path to Moel y Gest.

Cross straight over the road to another finger post and old kissing-gate. Pass through the gate and follow the good path to enter a lovely sessile oak wood with many bluebells in spring. The path ends at a track. Turn left down this to reach a 'Y' junction. Go down the left arm until the track shrinks to path. This continues to a dilapidated stile and broken fence. The path continues through woodland to reach a tarmac road descending between houses. Walk down this road ignoring two right turnings to a 'T' junction. Turn right into Borth y Gest reaching it at the road through the village. Cross straight over and turn left to the finger post for the Coastal Path.

There are good cafes in the village which can be reached very quickly by turning right.

Borth y Gest is a small, but lovely and quiet little village at the edge of the Glaslyn estuary. However, it once had a thriving ship building industry. In the period 1845 to 1880 thirty five ships were built. Pilot houses were built at the mouth of the harbour that enabled the pilots to keep a lookout for any ships that needed their help. Before Porthmadog was established Borth y Gest was the starting point for the dangerous crossing across Traeth Mawr to Harlech.

Turn right and follow the tarmac path away from the road going up spaced steps to join a road. Continue up this to a 'Y' junction. Bear right on the narrower road to where it descends to a boatyard on the right and a finger post. Continue ahead past several more small boatyards to a finger post at the start of a cobbled road and green with Porthmadog Marina to the right. Follow the cobbled road past Wharf House then turn right at the 'T' junction 100 metres further and continue to reach the main road through Porthmadog. Turn left. Continue through the town, passing many shops and an assortment of cafes, to a roundabout. Turn left and follow the road past the Aldi supermarket to the pull in.

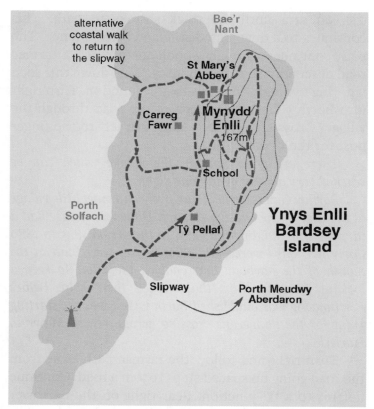

The summit of Mynydd Enlli

Walk 34
Mynydd Enlli

Walk details

Height:	*167 metres, Grid Ref. SH 1228 2193*
Distance:	*2½ miles by the South Ridge*
	2¼ miles by the direct approach
	2¾ miles returning via the coastal path
Time:	*At least 2½ hours for each of the first two walks or 3 hours for the coastal return*
O.S. Maps:	*1:25,000 Explorer Sheet 253 or*
	1:50,000 Landranger Sheet 123
Start:	*From the slipway on Ynys Enlli*
	Grid Ref. SH 1160 2109
Access:	*From Aberdaron drive to the car park for Porth Meudwy. Walk down the track to the slipway and catch your pre-booked boat journey to the island. Grid Ref. for car parking area SH 1591 2590*
Parking:	*Free*
Notes:	*A magnificent day out. The boat journey MUST be pre-booked*
Going:	*Tracks and grassy paths*

This is a magical adventure starting off with a 20–25 minutes boat ride from Porth Meudwy. Although this operates year round it is best to do this in the summer months when the sea is usually mirror smooth. Porth

Porth Meudwy

Meudwy is easily reached from Aberdaron. For up to date details and sailing times contact Colin Evans on 07971 769895. There is a short walk down to the slipway from the car parking area.

Whichever route is taken to the summit of Mynydd Enlli the views of the Llŷn peninsula from the summit are exceptional. The hill has an air of supremacy and the walk is a grand one indeed and the summit feels much higher than it is. I have described 2 routes up the hill. The one from the south is to be preferred as it has views most of the way. The other leads almost directly to the summit. I have described following the main track through the island back to the slipway as this passes through the isolated houses and by the bird observatory to reach Tŷ Pellaf where it is possible to have light refreshments such as tea, coffee and cakes. However, it is possible to follow the coastal path on the west side of the island across fields. I have not described this but left it for you to discover. NOTE: there is generally a 4 hours stay on the island. It is possible during exceptionally low tides some slippery scrambling is needed to get back on board the boat. A basic map is handed out by Colin on arrival on the island.

From the National Trust car park in Aberdaron turn left then left again and drive up the steep hill ignoring the turning right. There is a great view of Aberdaron near the top from a large pull in on the left. Continue to a road junction and turn left. Turn left at the sign for Porth Meudwy 800 metres further and drive down to the obvious left turn into the grassy car park at Cwrt. There are a couple of information panels here. From here it is necessary to walk down the track to the left to the slipway and the pretty bay of Porth Meudwy. This takes a very leisurely 10 minutes.

Ynys Enlli (Bardsey), is the legendary resting place of 20,000 saints. Whether all, or how many, of these actually were saints is not known. Many could well have been very religious people coming to the island to die! In a straight line from the tip of the headland it is less than 2 miles to the island. The waters between these points can be very dangerous with rip currents swirling, hence its Welsh name means 'the island of currents' whilst the English name indicates it is 'the island of Bards'. It could also refer to a Viking chief, Barda. The island is only 1 mile long and just over ½ mile wide.

It has long been a religious site. Saint Cadfan built a monastery here in 516 AD and was a major centre for pilgrimage. In fact it was said that three pilgrimages here were as good as one to Rome. The monastery was dissolved and demolished by Henry VIII in 1537. King Arthur is supposedly buried on the island.

Ynys Enlli became a National Nature Reserve in 1986. It is also a Site of Special Scientific Interest (SSSI). A very special bird associated with the island is the Manx shearwater with around 16,000 or so skulking in burrows during daylight hours. They sneak ashore under cover of darkness when there is preferably no moon. This represents around 5% of the total British population. They use abandoned rabbit burrows or make new ones to lay and hatch their eggs. There are no mainland predators such as rats or foxes, however because the shearwaters are clumsy on land they can fall prey to gulls.

The island is situated on a migratory route for birds flying to their breeding or wintering grounds. It is a bird watchers paradise when this happens with birds such as chiffchaffs, goldcrests, wheatears the first to pass through followed by sedge warblers, willow warblers, whitethroats and spotted flycatchers. Hundreds of seabirds use the eastern cliffs for nesting with guillemots, kittiwakes, razorbills and fulmars easily seen. One of the rarer birds here is the chough, a member of the crow family they are regarded as the Llŷn's bird. It is an exuberant bird with a mewing cry and an acrobatic flight. They have distinctive red legs, a red bill as well as being very black and glossy. In legend the soul of King Arthur migrated into the body of a chough after his last battle at Camlan near to Porth Ysgo. The red bill and legs were supposedly derived from the blood of that battle. It is said to be unlucky to kill this bird. Another rare bird is the little owl. Three or four pairs nest on the island in burrows due to the absence of trees that have hollows.

The island is one of the best places to spot grey seals with up to 200 or so sunbathing on islets in the summer with some 25 – 30 seal pups born each autumn. Dolphins and porpoises are often seen in the waters around the island. Marine life is unusually good. Clear waters encourage extensive growth of seaweed and because of it having a milder climate than the mainland species such as starfish, jewel anemone and cup coral can be found. Lobsters and crayfish are found offshore and 37 species of fish have been noted.

Botanists will also find much to interest them here as there are many rare lichens, some internationally so. In total there are over 350 recorded species. There are many flowers such as the rock sea lavender, small adder's tongue and western clover. One rarely seen flower is the purple loosestrife found only in very isolated places. An interesting insect known as the leafcutter bee is native. A native bee, it is so named on account of its remarkable ability to cut round circles in rose leaves. These are then used to seal the entrance to its nest.

Route 1 – Walk up the slipway and pass to the left of the boathouse bearing right to reach the track which passes through the middle of the island. Turn right and pass through the stone pillars. Go diagonally left across the field to pass through a gap in the fence followed by another and continue easily up with the fence on the left to reach a kissing-gate. Pass through this and turn left immediately and follow the path up, ignoring paths going off to the left towards Rhedynogoch to reach a broad grassy ridge. NOTE: DO NOT follow the path straight ahead at the kissing-gate. This passes around the headland and to the very steep and rocky east face. The path is very narrow and has much loose rock with some long vertical drops below it.

Turn left through a gap in the old stone and grass wall. The grassy path is easily followed up the broad south ridge although quite steeply avoiding several rock outcrops to the summit.

There are superb views from here towards the mainland. The three main headlands are easily seen and left to right these are Trwyn Gwyddel, Trwyn Bychestyn and Pen y Cil. Mynydd Mawr, 151 metres, with the white observation hut on the summit clearly seen above Trwyn

Gwyddel. Just to the right is Mynydd Anelog 192 metres. Yr Eifl form the skyline and in front of these and nearer is Garn Fadryn 371 metres and to the right again is the long ridge of Mynydd Rhiw 304 metres. The two small islands are Ynys Gwylan-fawr and Ynys Gwylan-fach. The mountains of Snowdonia look a very long way away indeed.

Route 2 – A shorter but much more direct way to approach the summit is to follow the main track. From the slipway reach the track as detailed above and continue up it to where it splits at an old limekiln. Turn left, right goes to Tŷ Pellaf where there is a craft shop and where light refreshments can be bought. Keep following the track and continue past a fine buttressed wall at Cristin, now the bird observatory to go through a gate. Turn up to the right 100 metres further opposite the next building, Plas Bach, on an obvious path. Go up to and through the kissing-gate.

Follow the clear path firstly to the right then left to zigzag up, ignoring the path out to the right towards a generator shed just after the start, to the summit ridge and a sudden view to die for. Turn left to the summit.

The remains of the abbey and the commemorative cross to Lord Newborough

To continue from the summit reached by whichever of the two routes is taken the walk continues by following the ridge northwards descending very gradually to almost reach the tip of the island. A steeper continuation descends more roughly then eases to cross some small springs before reaching and climbing over a hidden stile to the right of a house and left of a stone shed. Follow the path around to the left to reach the chapel. There is a great view of the abbey remains and the huge Celtic cross.

The chapel is always open and was built by Lord Newborough in 1875 who was the owner of the island at that time.

Turn right down the wide, grassy walled path to the track. Before turning left along the main track turn right to visit a lovely craft shop on the left of the track some 50 metres away. Opposite this are the remains of the old abbey and the large Celtic cross.

This commemorates Sir Spencer Bulkeley Wynn the 5th Baronet and 3rd Baron Newborough 21st May 1803 to 1st November 1888. His body was conveyed here on the 20th November 1889.

Turn back along the track and follow it to the limekiln and perhaps have a tea stop before returning to the slipway.

However, the walk can be extended by going through the waymarked gate on the left just beyond the craft shop and cross. Follow the path through the fields and coast back to the slipway having also visited the lighthouse.

This was built in 1821. It is unusual in that it is of a square construction and was designed by Daniel Alexander and built by Joseph Nelson.

Best Walks in Wales

A series of guide books to take you to every corner of this magnificent walking country

- Short family walks
- Excellent coastal walks
- Hill and mountain walks & panoramic views
- Level lakeside and valley walks
- Woodland and nature walks
- Fascinating heritage and history guides
- Clear coloured maps
- Route photos and attractions on the way
- Updated directions

www.carreg-gwalch.com

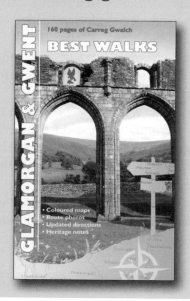

160 pages of Carreg Gwalch

BEST WALKS

ANGLESEY

* Coloured maps
* Route photos
* Updated directions
* Heritage notes

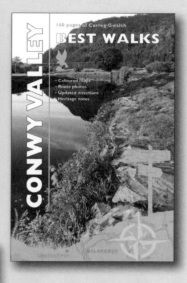

160 pages of Carreg Gwalch

BEST WALKS

CONWY VALLEY

* Coloured maps
* Route photos
* Updated directions
* Heritage notes

160 pages of Carreg Gwalch

BEST WALKS

LLŶN

* Coloured maps
* Route photos
* Updated directions
* Heritage notes

160 pages of Carreg Gwalch

BEST WALKS

CLWYDIAN RANGE

* Coloured maps
* Route photos
* Updated directions
* Heritage notes

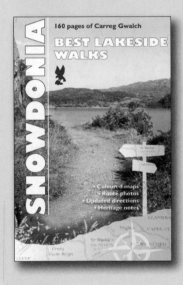

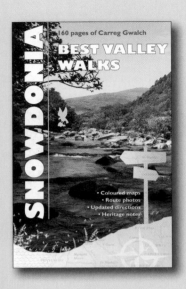

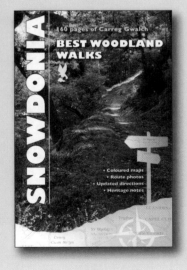